THE S

Current po

delegation to

growth alone: £271 billion per annum.
Nine out of 10 business owners would
reinvest their time in their businesses rather
than take time off if they could free up 10%
of their time. **More than 50% of business
owners believe they could grow their
business by more than 50% if they could
free up just 10% of their time.** More than
a third of business owners believe they should
delegate more. Two-thirds recognize the value
of delegation. **Time is the biggest barrier
to delegation and yet, ironically, this
is what delegation saves
most of.**[1]

[1]Statistics published as part of the appended White Paper (Appendix 1of this book) and
Manifesto (Appendix 2 of this book), which were the first publications surrounding my research
into delegation, initial thinking on value and benefit of delegation and my thoughts on how to
capitalize on this.

'A combination of research and practical experience make this well-written book invaluable for those struggling to effectively delegate and manage a team.'

Julie Gledhill, Finance Director, hoyhoy.nl

'Anyone wanting to take control over their life, enjoying the work that they do, continuously, needs this "Gift". The online programme also brings the whole subject to life.'

Simon North, Founder of Position Ignition

'Businesses succeed when they delegate, spreading responsibility and autonomy upwards, downwards and sideways. Gail Thomas's extensive personal experience translates into valuable words of wisdom on what we might soon call "the art of delegating".'

Julian Barling, PhD FRSC, Borden Chair of Leadership & Author of *The Science of Leadership*

THE GIFT OF TIME

HOW DELEGATION CAN GIVE YOU SPACE TO SUCCEED

GAIL THOMAS

CAPSTONE
A Wiley Brand

This edition first published 2015
© 2015 Gail Thomas

Registered office
John Wiley and Sons Ltd, The Atrium, Southern Gate, Chichester, West Sussex, PO19 8SQ,
United Kingdom

For details of our global editorial offices, for customer services and for information about
how to apply for permission to reuse the copyright material in this book please see our
website at www.wiley.com.

Wiley publishes in a variety of print and electronic formats and by print-on-demand. Some
material included with standard print versions of this book may not be included in e-books
or in print-on-demand. If this book refers to media such as a CD or DVD that is not
included in the version you purchased, you may download this material at
http://booksupport.wiley.com. For more information about Wiley products, visit
www.wiley.com.

Designations used by companies to distinguish their products are often claimed as
trademarks. All brand names and product names used in this book and on its cover are trade
names, service marks, trademarks or registered trademarks of their respective owners. The
publisher and the book are not associated with any product or vendor mentioned in this
book. None of the companies referenced within the book have endorsed the book.

Limit of Liability/Disclaimer of Warranty: While the publisher and author have used their
best efforts in preparing this book, they make no representations or warranties with respect
to the accuracy or completeness of the contents of this book and specifically disclaim any
implied warranties of merchantability or fitness for a particular purpose. It is sold on the
understanding that the publisher is not engaged in rendering professional services and
neither the publisher nor the author shall be liable for damages arising herefrom. If
professional advice or other expert assistance is required, the services of a competent
professional should be sought.

Library of Congress Cataloging-in-Publication Data is available

A catalogue record for this book is available from the British Library.

ISBN 978-0-857-08595-5 (pbk)
ISBN 978-0-857-08594-8 (ebk) ISBN 978-0-857-08593-1 (ebk)

Cover Design and Illustration: Wiley

Set in 11/15pt MinionPro by Aptara Inc., New Delhi, India
Printed in Great Britain by TJ International Ltd, Padstow, Cornwall, UK

CONTENTS

CONTENTS

Part Four   Delegation in context

INTRODUCTION

A whole book on the subject of delegation? Who'd have thought?

Personally, I love short paragraphs and chapters: I'm a total 'cut to it' person. No fluff required. If you're like that too, here's your reason to stick with this book, even though it's longer than an article:

There's loads in it for you, to make other things shorter and your life better.

If you need a bit more, here's the next part:

- Delegation is a multi-media, multi-directional necessity of life (how thoroughly modern of me).

- There are many benefits to getting delegation right in life: at home as well as at work.

- The potential of successful delegation to the UK economy at just under £300 billion per annum – you should take your share of that.

- I know that clients I've dealt with are usually disappointed that there is no quick fix. Great delegation takes time (for many reasons TIME is the biggest barrier to successful delegation) but the benefits are MASSIVE – I'm a real live case study and I talk about it readily at the drop of a hat.

A grandiose and somewhat unachievable sound bite from Vince Cable at MADE Festival for start-up businesses in 2012 was the inspiration for this book. He said, and I paraphrase, 'If we had 900 000 new businesses in the UK tomorrow, we would not have an economic problem. Unemployment would be reduced to an acceptable level, the economic deficit would be eradicated and our future pensions problem would be resolved.'

As a serial starter of businesses, I found what he said massively appealing, but as one who knows how tricky it is to get going in the first place, let alone keep a young business afloat, I knew in truth it was a big, if not impossible, ask.

But the maths intrigued me and wouldn't let me go. I knew that the UK at that point had some 4.5 million businesses and thus 900 000 as a proportion of that was 20%. So, give or take, if the businesses that we already had grew by 20%, one could presume that the net effect on the economy would be the same.

So how does a business go about growing by 20%? All manner of ways, I suspect: brand extension, product development, asset leverage, marketing sales, economies of scale, process-reengineering, social media and business development. It matters not, to be honest. Growth takes time and money, but mainly time – especially if you've just come out of a recession and the banks aren't lending!

So if growth, enough to eradicate our economic woes (ref Vince Cable), takes time from those with the skills to create it, then – I figured – the only way to give these people the time they need is to reduce their workload. The only way to make this happen is by delegating; and if that is true, it de facto means there is value in delegation.

So I asked the question: 'If you could reduce your workload by 10%, what would you do with the time?'

Over 90% of respondents from SMEs said they would grow the business.

And so I asked them how much by. Somewhat ironically, given the Vince Cable starting point, the average response was always just over 20%.

Then if you take the current government statistics on SMEs alone and apply the figures to owner-led businesses, the resulting expected growth, on delegating 10% of workload alone, is almost £300 billion per annum.

So if you were wondering how this book got its title, there you are.

For those who like the greater explanation, here's your bit:

Mastering the art of delegation is so much more than that, more than 'just' more money. There is much written on delegation in many media and forms and I'm sure I've only touched the very outside in my own reading. What I've seen, though, doesn't differ from the bits of delegation theory that I read when I studied for my MBA. It's absolutely right in its content but it's less compelling if it isn't clear why you might partake. Let me expand here, because this is the nub of the justification of one whole book dedicated to the single subject of delegation.

In a corporate sense, I often find it's simply a management skill that is expected, sits theoretically in the lower echelons of the managerial skill set and yet is rarely taught or trained in. Less, or even never, is it valued as a benefit to the organization in financial or managerial terms. In my experience, it is usually positioned as a skill which benefits team motivation; trite acronyms accompany an expectation that rank will facilitate necessary delegation. 'I am more senior, therefore I will pass my workload to you and you will enjoy and feel motivated by the additional responsibility because it says you are trusted and worthy.' I'm simplifying and exaggerating to make a point here, but the MBA I studied didn't give much more than this, to be honest.

It took some time for me to realize I had been in the business of delegation for well over a decade; sharing my secretary with others to save costs led to a small business that was established in 2001 not just surviving, but still going strong well into its second decade. Every visit to that office reinforces the relief that business owners and department managers must or would feel when they hear those words, 'Leave it with me, I'll sort it out for you.' It makes my heart dance. Even more so when the person being delegated to loves the prospect of helping out by doing work they love.

There is a hugely pleasant feeling that accompanies successful delegation but it is most definitely a habit and, for some people, it's a bit like developing the habit of exercise or going to the gym. It takes effort to break the barrier of not delegating and doing it for oneself. Overcome that barrier and the upside worms its way into the psyche, which makes it addictive because the benefits are so evident.

I focus a lot on time being the biggest benefit of delegation, with the proviso that what you do with it is the ergo benefit(s). However, as delegation always works laterally, it is possible to collaborate and redistribute work according to who is good at, or loves, doing certain things, so it can also mean that you get to do more of what you're great at and presumably love doing most.

In addition, it means that you're surrounded by people who are doing the stuff that you're not good at, and we know that that is a winning strategy. Always get someone who is better than you to do stuff for you: it means a better job gets done – if ever there was a no-brainer, how much encouragement do you need?

Either way, delegation means you get to fill more of your time with stuff you want to do, as opposed to being overwhelmed with things you don't like doing so much, which therefore take longer to do and longer to mentally move away from once done, and in doing so cost even more time. That's a mouthful, but it's true.

This book is intended to get the message out there that sharing, or in other words delegating downwards, upwards and sideways, is good for us individually, as a family, as a team, as a small business, as a department, as a big business and thus as an economy. I don't think we do it enough, I don't think we're taught how to do it or that it is a good thing to do and I'm hoping this book, the accompanying online programme and the available workshops help to change that.

Good luck. Delegate and grow.

Part One
INTRODUCING DELEGATION

1
THE DEFINITION
OF DELEGATION

M ost people walk around with knowledge of many words and probably wouldn't feel a need to look them up in a dictionary. I only looked up the verb 'delegate' myself for the sake of clarity at the beginning of a workshop I was about to deliver. I almost didn't recognize the word from its definition. In fact, I realized that the word's meaning had changed and that it was time to revisit the notion of delegation with a fresh pair of eyes, to revisit this often ignored – though always expected – skill of a manager.

The strict definition as written in the *Oxford English Dictionary* is:

To delegate *vb* the act of transferring or handing over work to another person usually more junior than oneself.

This was probably highly appropriate and factually correct during the fifties, sixties and maybe even seventies, when a secretary was often the equivalent of an 'office wife', the 'boss' was more-often called by title and surname and subordinates by their first or surname only. Management status was cherished and the notion of rank still fresh from the post-war era. The eighties perpetuated the notion of delegation as a one-way process, the sometimes-aggressive dumping of often less attractive tasks to a junior.

The characteristic excess and status-led attitude of the yuppie years gave way to a much more sensitive and somewhat politically-correct era which led to a far greater consideration of managerial relationships and the dynamics of emotional intelligence being applied in the workplace.

In addition, during this time, essentially from the nineties onwards, we have seen an explosion in technological advancement. Though the eighties was the beginning of the mobile phone era, the nineties saw the rise of email and electronic communication, and thereafter and through the noughties, we have seen the rise of social networking sites and more latterly the (largely worldwide) addition of smartphones.

Smartphones have to a great extent imprisoned us in a world of infomania, whereby the phone has become a constant companion, less a phone for many and more a device that makes unqualified demands on our time. As a consequence it is a huge distraction, often dragging highly-paid and highly-qualified professionals and business people into a time-wasting mire of deletion and (often over-zealous, ill-considered) speedy responses. Of course, emails, social media and the Internet are hugely valuable too, but their impact on delegation, in the strict sense of the word, has been dramatic.

Think back to the archetypal image of a secretary who, for the sake of stereotypical accuracy, we will say was female. Her role was to take down dictation, type up letters and memos (remember them?), often she would draft replies to letters and memos herself, in her boss's style for *him* to edit and/or sign. For him, his communication schedule was controlled and limited: the post came in and was prioritized for his attention by his secretary. Communiqués requiring urgent attention were pushed under his nose, with or without suggested replies. He studied them, decided how to act, dictated or directed a responsive action to his secretary (reply, meeting, delegation to another or ignore) and got on with other things until she had something to report. Note then that he was not constantly checking for replies or in fact able to directly communicate quickly or instigate prolonged, often instant, discussion on a matter.

Clearly this scenario rarely exists today, but its historic place in our, actually quite recent view, of delegation remains true. Fast forward even to the nineties and I would argue that secretaries were far more likely to be in charge of the email inbox, responding on behalf of their managers, deleting, prioritizing, replying and taking action where appropriate, precisely as a result of the legacy of a life and role prior to the emergence of electronic communication.

My point here is not to make or even attempt to make a social study on the impact that the digital age has had on our lives and economy. Far from it: merely, I seek to illustrate that roles have changed in recent times as a result of these advances and with it our certainty and our relationship with skills such as delegation.

If I may stray briefly from the management skill that is delegation, let us expand the notion that the social digital age has blurred the lines for many of us and that adaptation is vital to maintain quality leadership in our businesses and successful businesses as a result. Our lives are now indelibly published online, see the enlightening short talk by Juan Enriquez.[1] They can be researched by employers assessing potential and in-post employees and vice versa. Managers can no longer maintain a professional distance from their colleagues, team and managers, unless they entirely shun the social media world and, even then, they have limited control over what others may post about them, pictures and all. This changes the game. Managerial leadership now has to be managed in the context of an extended professional landscape. Everyone can have a deeper knowledge of anyone else's personal or past professional life, all at the push of a button. Suddenly we are all 'famous'. If, once again, we take the strict definition of the word,[2] then without qualification of the elements 'known' and 'many' we all have the potential to fall into the category of famous, and so we have to add reputation management more vigorously to our skill portfolio.

These days many of us grapple, at all ages, to understand what this alone means to our online persona: How we appear to everyone in our world; friends, family, our children and their

---

[1] *Ted Talk: Your online life, permanent as a tattoo*, http://www.ted.com/talks/juan_enriquez_how_to_think_about_digital_tattoos, accessed 10th October 2014.
[2] *Oxford English Dictionary* definition of 'fame': 'mass noun; the state of being known by many people'.

grandchildren, their teachers and lecturers, our employers, colleagues, suppliers and clients is increasingly something to think about. And we have a very clear and present need to address what this means for each of us. As an entrepreneurial middle-aged female with pre-teen children, I have both a business and personal need to understand these technological impacts, but I am not a 'techy': I find it more a necessary evil than a welcome invasion. That said, I embrace the benefits into my life without thinking about them – instant messaging, online diary and document access, indulgent voyeurism, music and movies on the move and so on. My chances of being 'papped' in a compromising Friday night position by a 'friend' who then plasters the pics all over the latest social media platform are mercifully limited (though not entirely over!); however, management of these risks for our children are highly prevalent and relevant. The benefits and damage – even to the point of suicide – are extreme and real and in large part we all understand the need to learn to deal with it.

More importantly, though, with regards to this book, we need to understand what, sometimes subtle, impacts this new, modern, technology-driven world has on delegation – how we delegate, how often, what form it takes and how effective it is. These impacts are not just the preserve of technology, though its existence influences the other key factors of gender and (slowly) increasing equality between the sexes and the influence of culture on this.

If we look again at the post-war period, we will see the stereotype of a white-collar male worker making his way up the corporate ladder and the point when he would be awarded the 'office wife'.

This would be a benefit both for him and for his real-life wife, as the new employee would be able to do more personal tasks for their boss – such as picking up the dry-cleaning, making hair and dental appointments – that normally fell to the boss's housewife. This was the social, status and professional reward for achieving a certain level of management.

These days, where the equivalent of the 'office wife' exists in a less frequent/more likely to be shared scenario and with the advent of greater equality, greater expectations of women's performance and career ambitions in the workplace, the delegation relationship is often (but not yet always) very different.

Culturally, we live in a more equal society where the media has helped to shape our views of those in positions of so-called power. Celebrities, royals and politicians are regularly featured and exposed in publications and online; in fact as social media enables us to instantly enter almost anyone's life, a degree of deference has almost certainly been lost at all levels of society.

And so delegation, in part, becomes a choice not just for the superior, to draw on the *Oxford English Dictionary* definition and to return us to the original point, but also for the junior. It is less an expected part of one's lot and more an acceptable part of one's role. That it is acceptable also means it can be deemed unacceptable and this, to my mind, defines the art of delegation or, more precisely, the verb 'to delegate', as a skill that involves reducing one's own workload by handing it over to another party (or software) application who (that) agrees to execute an agreed list of actions to an agreed standard within an agreed time.

Later, we will apply this thinking to delegation in scenarios other than the workplace and examine the multi-directional and multi-media capability of delegation in the home and in a political landscape as well as looking more deeply at the upwards and sideways manifestations of delegation.

The Gift of Time is accompanied by an online programme that offers practical help, activities and accountability for action.[3]

---

[3] For more information see: http://thegiftoftime.yourgoalstoday.com/.

2
THE BENEFITS OF DELEGATION

There are multiple benefactors of successful or even simply effective delegation when it is an integral part of a company's operational culture.

We will address the financial benefits which apply to business owners, or those responsible and directly able to influence company growth, later; but in the meantime, what about everyone and everything else? Where are the benefits for them and what do they look like, and how – most importantly – can this be measured? As well as what I term 'soft benefits', which relate to how people feel in their work and in their life, there are also 'hard benefits', which can directly transcribe into financial improvement. It's a (somewhat sad) fact of life that money talks. In terms of adopting a new way of working (i.e. delegating more and the encouragement to do so in a corporate environment), there has to be a clear benefit to the organization, something more than 'hope value'. The prospect of generating an increase of cold hard cash is always a good motivator, and therein lies the importance of the value of delegation in financial terms.

Whatever the varied benefits of delegation, there is one common denominator which results from effective delegation: time. By virtue of handing over workload or tasks, the delegator first gets his or her time back. This is the benefit of delegation. In truth, it is the only benefit of delegation to the delegator, what then transpires may or may not be a beneficial use of that time, but time in itself provides the benefit of choice.

Clearly, if one operates as a business owner or at the top of an organization and with limited supervision, the choice of what to do with time freed up is arguably greater. If the 'why' which motivates the delegation in the first place is clear, agreed and achievable then the benefits become more recognizable and tangible as they manifest. If the 'why' is not clear – and we will tackle this in greater depth as part of the process of delegation – then time can easily be wasted, and we are all capable of that.

If delegation in its strictest sense is passing on work to someone else and if the immediate and most obvious result of that is an unfilled gap in time, let's look at where that could lead in the following diagram (Figure 2.1).

If we back-pedal a little, we can start at home with the young. The purpose of a parent is to make themselves redundant. There is more on this – with commentary from Elizabeth O'Shea, a renowned parenting coach – in Chapter 14. In achieving their own redundancy, parents (and clearly within this term I include any form of carer) produce young adults, capable, independent and equipped, insofar as they can be, to take on the world of adulthood.

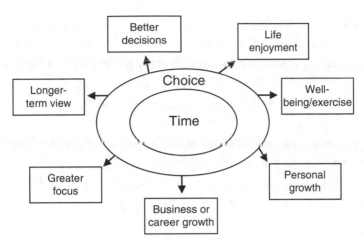

Figure 2.1   Delegation benefits map.

The result, of course, will be happier, more independent children who know that part of their role is to pass on this knowledge to future generations.

And if we start to achieve 'redundancy' at work, we will create a rolling production line of passing back the workload, tasks and required outcomes, freeing up time for us to develop, grow and find new ways of achieving more, and being more fulfilled.

There are many routes and stakeholders and there are many motivating reasons for making oneself redundant; retirement, for example, is most successfully achieved for both the individual and the organization if a successor who picks up the workload and carries forth the legacy of the retiree is put into place. The retiree is free to retire because he or she is effectively redundant, by design of course.

Similarly, an employee leaving a role or an organization is a fact of life and a fact of a successful career. Just as in the case of our retiree, leaving a role is much more successfully achieved if the role leaver has been able to achieve their own 'redundancy' through the appointment and training of a successor.

Great delegation creates jobs at the back end of the production line and development, improvement and breakthroughs at the front line. One can't possibly do all that one already does and then add in more in order to improve or progress.

The ability to delegate with the intention of making the initial job description as redundant as possible

- creates employment, directly and virtually

- means flexible working and new self-employment opportunities for otherwise 'unemployable' people[1]

- enables employees at all levels to delegate those areas of their workload that are least favourable, that they're less good at or that they can pass on to a potential successor so that they can add new skills, take on or develop new activities or explore new ways to improve their self, job,

---

[1] By 'unemployable' I do not mean no one wants to employ them by virtue of anything they are or have done, rather that culturally it is not possible for them to take up work on the terms that they are currently able to offer, e.g. mothers who do not want to work full time but cannot get employment part time with the flexibility to accommodate school holidays, child sickness etc. Or increasingly members of the older generation who are unable to afford full-time retirement or to operate well in a full-time capacity and thus have reduced working hours, yet possess a wealth of experience and skills for organizations to draw upon.

team or organization, i.e. have a better and more enjoyable job and so be a better and more pleasant co-worker

- enables managers and executives to explore the limits of their potential because they are not bogged down by repetitive tasks through downward delegation

- enables employees at all levels to develop their skill sets and experience and to earn accolades and show their potential to their superiors through successful upward delegation as well as successful receipt of downward delegated workload

- enables a happier workforce comprising workers who play to their strengths through sideways delegation and get to enjoy jobs that consist largely of things they enjoy doing most and are best at.

Economic impacts spread far:

- In creating employment, we create increased disposable income and an increase in consumerism as well as all the related impacts on the housing and property market.

- In freeing up SME owners to create growth, we already know of the hundreds of billions of pounds this adds to the global economy.

- In freeing up managers and executives to be creative and generate growth, we naturally return increased taxes to the government and improve shareholder return (which also presumably results in bonuses for staff in all the requisite benefits mentioned above regarding disposable income).

- In applying all the same delegation disciplines and in achieving all the same results in civil service, government and government divisions, we achieve improvements in service delivery and through reduction in costs underlying a return or benefit to the taxpayer.

- In applying all the same to charities, an increased proportion of funds raised can be attributed – one hopes – to the causes supported by the charity.

3
THE VALUE OF DELEGATION

There are many 'soft benefits' to delegation which arc high-lighted in the previous chapter but there is a definitive commercial value to the bottom line of a business or organization that gets delegation right. It manifests itself essentially in four ways:

- the newly-created revenue – for SMEs, corporate, charities and governments (discussed more below);

- the value added to the business – for SMEs as a reduction of dependence on the owner, both for resale and for business resilience;

- the value added to the business as a result of removal of the owner from the day-to-day operation of the business;

- the savings made on staff salaries and benefits as a result of reduction of tasks carried out by over-qualified staff.

Newly-created revenue as a result of delegation

It was only this first that I set out to measure when I started my studies and research into the art of delegation. The basic premise was a simple one: if, in this first instance, a business owner could free up 10% of their time, what would they do with that time? Of the first two hundred respondents, over 90% of them had 'grown their business' in their results. Asked how much by, the average level was over 20%. So a workload reduction of 10% would result in a business growth of 20%.

It was simple then to pick up government statistics on SMEs and their turnover and extrapolate what a 20% uplift across the board would mean to the economy. The result can be measured in billions, £271 billion pounds per annum to be precise.

This figure, of course, represents potential only: business owners may not achieve their 20% growth, they may struggle to free up 10% of their time and keep it that way or they may do something else with the time, like semi-retire or just keep the business ticking over. But what is clear is that for a focused owner who delegates sensibly and well the value is manifold.

And for the economy as a whole, a growth in business of 20% has manifest benefits: there will be more individuals with disposable income and more individuals being taxed, benefiting both the High Street and the nation as a whole.

But the 10% workload has to go somewhere, and here is a further benefit: delegation results in increased employment and/or an inherent uplift in the requirement for a virtual or flexible work-force (i.e. the virtual assistant, or VA, market), which allows individuals to offer their time for money and thus gives an entry back into the workplace where before there was none.

For a one-person business with a turnover of, say, £60,000 per annum who frees up 10% of their time and creates growth of 20% as a result, their income is increased by £1000 per month. To a small business with £400k turnover – £80k and a larger business with a turnover of £2.5m – the potential uplift as a result of delegation – more than half a million pounds.

In corporates with a mission to grow, the potential for growth is amazing. This is something that wasn't entirely expected when I started my research. One of my early clients had a very clear objective: to free up partner time – all 150 of them – and enable them to get out from behind the desk and get networking in a bid to grow their client base and so bill more hours. To achieve this would amount to millions of pounds of turnover. Within minutes of the first workshop, tens of thousands of pounds had been saved in billable time through a new process that had been delegated.

A programme of education executed with the junior partners and senior associates in the same firm meant that the delegators could more easily delegate to an engaged team who in turn had teams to delegate to and each other, through identified strengths to delegate in a sideways fashion (see Chapter 7).

It's a pleasure to work through a training programme or syllabus topic and help a whole organization see that they can delegate and grow, be delegated to and grow and enjoy their role with happier colleagues, relieved managers and enthused teams.

It is appreciated of course that delegation may not, without all the accompanying skills, produce the value in terms of growth, and this is a separate factor not addressed in this book. Skills surrounding sales, marketing, client service, operations, finance and cash management are of course critical to business success, but it is nonetheless difficult to dispute that there is no inherent value in the art of delegation.

Value created by the reduction of dependence on, or removal of, the owner of the business

A former client who remains a friend recently said she'd love to franchise her business. She started up in the late nineties and her business has served her well: she has privately educated her family, has a lovely home and owns the business premises. The problem was, she told me, no one would be mad enough to do what she did. I naturally asked what she did, and the answer was so much work that she was in work six days a week all year round with two weeks off at Christmas and two weeks in the summer.

True. Long hours are not for everyone. And so there she was, with premises that she owned (i.e. perfect to lease to the buyer of her business), with a business that few would ever really want to buy as, by her own admission, she had no life and so neither would her successor. She couldn't really offer her business for sale and should anything happen to her the business would immediately fail, there would be no get-out of the building with its current use class and her family would face significant financial hardship.

Delegation, even to the uninitiated, is the obvious answer. For a number of reasons:

If she delegated, even just some of the workload, my friend would have a better life, be less exhausted and perhaps be able to think about that holy grail – franchise. This is a perfect example of the benefit of delegation when the 'Why' is clear.

If she delegated, there would be a natural potential stand-in for her role, someone who at least would have a fighting chance of understanding just what she did as the owner and sole employee. This would give the business some resilience in the event of absence following sickness, injury or for any other reason. By 'resilience', I mean continued revenue from continued business operations, which would enable the business owner to receive some income even in the event of her temporary absence.

If she delegated, and there was more than one person with knowledge of her business's operations, the business would increase its saleability, because it would be possible to buy the business, keep the founder on to train up her replacement(s) before ultimately replacing her. Suddenly, the business would go from a guaranteed closedown to the possibility, at least, of some revenue from a sale. The business owner could at least expect the equivalent of a year's profit in return for a fully operational business should she decide to sell.

If she could largely remove herself from the business to the point where all she did was manage it, preferably at a higher rate of pay, the profit to earnings ratio applied in the sale valuation would be so much higher and so more comparable to the going market rate.

If my friend could remove herself entirely, or almost entirely, and see the business operate successfully without her, she could have a franchise-able model and untold potential, whether she franchised or not, to sell her business at a premium rate. This is because a potential buyer would have either no or a limited need to learn about the business for themselves. Their return would not be in the salary plus profits of the business owner but in the profit of a business which had the capacity and processes to grow, without their direct involvement (i.e. one could attract investors expecting a return rather than business buyers who wanted a job plus some profit in return for their investment).

Valuing delegation in corporate, charities and government departments

Conversely, when we look at larger organizations, the financial benefits of delegation appear to come at first from the savings made on paying over-qualified staff members. Often, especially when times are tough and finances tight, the first thing to be cut is the salary budget. Not to say this is a bad thing, but often what happens is that the support staff are culled without sufficient thought to the impacts on management and more senior staff. Either that or, as headcount reductions start, natural wastage kicks in and in some cases the most talented staff leave. Or it can simply be a case of natural financial caution that a highly qualified member of staff is required to carry out tasks that do not justify his or her level of pay and could quite easily be carried out by a junior member of staff.

I am aware that this can sound like I'm pandering to the 'higher ups' and that financial constraints are not the only reason delegation sometimes does not happen. We cover barriers in a later chapter, but for this one the point here is the value that results from delegation when it happens well.

Delegation in larger businesses (as well actually as in smaller businesses) generates financial benefit in two ways: first, on the difference in salary between the manager and the subordinate and, second, on the higher-level work which results from the freed-up time. This all of course assumes that delegation happens well and that everyone works optimally, but even those industries that in theory should completely get the 'time equals money' equation, because it is their fundamental business model, fall foul of the value that sensible delegation brings. This is no more starkly and ironically illustrated than in professional firms (law, accountancy, etc.) and has been prevalent through the tougher times of recent years, when these industries' senior staff, in a bid to maintain billable hours, begin to hoard work that could and should be delegated. This results in their working to capacity and being less freed up to develop new business through existing or new clients. At the same time, the junior level below them, associate or manager level, are less occupied and fewer roles at this level are available. The ratio between this level and their support staff is therefore increased and an obvious place to cut costs (support level) becomes available. A vicious circle pretty much results, which evolves into a cycle of negative feedback:

- Less new business.

- Existing business starts to drop off as hours are billed at higher level and money is already tight.

- Middle-level jobs are fewer, resulting in lower salaries and underused, demotivated, underdeveloped junior managers, who ultimately could drop out of the industry altogether.

- Support staff feel under pressure and undervalued.

Tighter financial times naturally result in shorter-term views where costs are under scrutiny and sometimes the lowest-hanging fruit is the easiest to divest, but this is not necessarily the best way to go. Sales and (effective) marketing should never stop, in any market, and if it is possible to free up the time of a company's most likely business-makers through delegation, then this is one way to maintain a longer-term view of a more sustainable future and is preferable to making short-term cuts at the support team level.

What is clear to me is that building a culture, attracting and retaining talent, system and product innovation, product and channel extensions and strategic plans and scale infrastructure all take time. Time is freed up, especially for business founders used to running the business, through the art of effective delegation.

Mirroring this below the line, it is generally a lack of time that leads to mismanaged costs, reliance on one source of revenue, poor team management and an inability to react and respond to external influences on the marketplace.

Delegate and regain the time; delegate and generate the choice; delegate and generate the value. I am pleased to include here an article by Peter Harford, CEO of Assay Advisory, a company which helps businesses and business owners to increase their valuation and prepare for sale or exit.

Increasing the pre-sale value of your business

Source: Reproduced by kind permission of Assay Advisory

Beyond profitability

Profit growth usually tops the agenda for mid-tier businesses wanting to increase pre-sale valuation. But this common approach to increasing a business's equity value often takes substantial effort. For example, in initiatives such as lifting sales through recruitment and training or opening new premises.

While profitability is an important influence on a business's equity value, it is not the only determinant.

We regularly help clients increase the value *already present* in their business through a focus on assets, in addition to profits. Without an asset understanding, mid-tier businesses tend to favour a purely finance-based valuation. This means many owners lose a vital opportunity to increase value and therefore undersell their businesses.

The valuation equation

Most owners are familiar with the business valuation equation: $V = P \times M$, where the valuation (V) of a business equals profit (P) times a multiple (M). If profit is £10m and the valuation multiple is five, then the company is valued at £50m.

The multiple is simply a measure and judgement of future profits. The greater the likelihood of future profits the higher the multiple, while a low probability reduces it.

Sounds easy in principle, but there is more behind this apparent simplicity.

The finance-based approach to valuing a mid-tier business is retrospective, typically averaging the last three to five years' profits and applying a financial rate of return. Effectively the buyer purchases an historic cash flow where the multiple ties into the likelihood – the risk – of that cash flow continuing.

This accounting approach is widespread and a legitimate business valuation method. But an alternative approach focuses on the valuation multiple rather than profit alone.

Understanding the multiple

In general, industries each have an industry multiple norm. Businesses in the same industry with similar market share, turnover and profitability would typically attract the same multiple – the norm or what we call the 'line'.

The traditional finance-based valuation approach starts on the 'line' and then looks 'below the line' for risks that justify lowering the multiple and therefore the value. In other words, discount the multiple because the business risks suggest future profits are uncertain.

We call this a 'two dimensional' valuation approach.

Instead we adopt a prospective, asset-based approach. While we do look retrospectively at profits, we are equally as interested in what the business will make in the future.

Use your assets

Our 'third dimension' approach reveals what exists 'above the line', the so-called off-balance sheet assets. These are not necessarily present on a typical balance sheet alongside equipment, property, vehicles etc. Off-balance sheet assets may not have generated profits historically, but will do so in the future. Or more importantly, they will generate future profits in the hands of a strategic acquirer.

Take the tech company that never made a profit yet still sold for millions of dollars. While the company may not have made a profit, perhaps the asset is a large user-base through which a strategic acquirer could sell its own products or services.

This buyer would therefore pay an equity value that ignores the company's historical profits. In this case the business has gained a higher multiple – increased likelihood of future profits – and therefore attracts a higher overall valuation.

Above/below the line

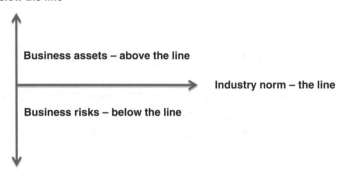

- Business assets – above the line
- Industry norm – the line
- Business risks – below the line

Increase the multiple

Case studies show businesses adopting an asset-based approach to valuation sell for significantly more than their industry multiple norm. A traditional finance-based acquirer will typically only pay a four or five times norm, but the strategic acquirer will pay a higher valuation multiple. The business has not changed in these cases, but the buyer's perspective regarding the business (and the multiple) has.

We often find clients have created business assets with a profit motive and therefore do not value them strategically. For example, imagine your business has developed a truly innovative system to increase margins and volume through process efficiency – a profit motive.

A strategic acquirer, rather than a traditional finance-based buyer, will be interested in your system because they can apply it to their other businesses. Adopting an asset-based approach in this way increases the multiple and therefore the valuation of your business.

Less energy required

When working with our mid-tier business clients, we begin by discussing their initiatives to increase valuation before sale. Understandably people tend to focus on the 'P' aspect of $V = P \times M$ because they know how to influence profit.

Clients often say, 'If I increase profits then I'll get my valuation up.' While this is true, it misses the other valuation lever – the multiple. While business owners know that profit equals volume times margin, they typically do not have the same level of understanding about the multiple formula.

During the valuation conversation, we explain how a client's (typically off-balance sheet) assets have the potential to increase future profits while identifying any factors that will reduce them. In other words, what business 'above the line' features should be recognised and formalised? In addition, what 'below the line' issues present risks to future profits and must therefore be addressed?

Our aim is to increase awareness around the assets you have, but perhaps do not currently recognise as such – assets with the potential to attract a strategic acquirer and increase your multiple.

Instead of struggling to increase profitability, increasing the multiple takes less energy. Why? Because you have probably created assets already that will attract a strategic buyer.

How an asset-based process works

Supporting a business through an asset-based approach to valuation can be summarised in three steps.

Step 1: Value the business today

Business owners do not typically have an accurate idea of their current business valuation. This leaves them feeling reactive and hoping they have something that will eventually be saleable.

As a first step, a pro-forma valuation gives the owner an objective valuation of their business. This moves them from reactive to proactive by providing information about the start point for building on the business's equity valuation.

Step 2: Determine the exit vision

Step two determines a detailed exit vision, which involves defining both the valuation and timing of exit. While owners often have an idea of their targeted valuation at exit, they rarely have a deconstructed formula to arrive at that figure.

For example, a business with an exit vision of a £100m valuation could achieve this with either option below:

$$P \times M = V$$

Option 1: £20m $\times$ 5 = £100m

Option 2: £10m $\times$ 10 = £100m

Each of these options requires a significantly different strategy to be implemented.

Step 3: Design an equity enhancement program

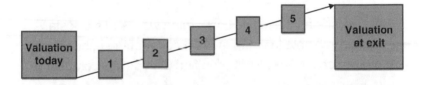

Step three identifies the stepping stones to move a business from its current valuation to its targeted exit valuation. These stepping stones are a combination of strategic projects/initiatives and potential interim transactions.

Specific focus is given to strategic projects/initiatives that will enhance the business's valuation multiple. These are identified during the detailed 'above/below the line' analysis explained earlier.

During these three steps clients become more aware of assets within their business that will attract a strategic

THE GIFT OF TIME

(rather than financial) acquirer. Armed with this information, and increased knowledge of strategic investor language, clients are more confident and effective in conducting sale negotiations. Now they can offer more than historical profits alone.

Proactively groom your business for sale

The market for mid-tier business sales during the 2008-2012 global financial crisis was extremely flat. However, now that economic conditions are improving, previously unsold stock is re-entering the market. Coupled with this fact, the retiring baby boomer generation is also looking to sell its mid-tier businesses in ever increasing numbers.

We are seeing these two converging waves of stock starting to come onto the market. As a consequence, business owners looking to sell will soon find themselves competing in a very busy space.

If you are looking to sell your business, how will you stand out in this increasingly crowded market?

Understanding the assets that sit within your business – and will attract a strategic acquirer – places you in a far better position than looking to sell using a traditional financial valuation approach.

Inspired by the Assay model, we can assume that if the current management team have not delegated at least some of their day-to-day workload then they are unlikely to effectively deliver the strategy. Without succession and clear training and support programmes in place, delegation is unlikely to be successful.

If revenue is well distributed across clients and product streams then risk to the future business is reduced and profitability is at least safeguarded if not increased. Creating and delivering new revenue streams in the first place requires time and creative thought as well as operational planning.

Creating a great place to work with a queue to get in is a hugely attractive proposition to an acquirer. Creating such a culture, coaching and nurturing the talent that joins, all requires time.

Innovation, as well as creativity, takes research, which, as mentioned, also takes time. While existing assets and client bases are clearly leveraged to deliver such innovation, it can still be as time-consuming and preoccupying as creating an entirely new business all over again. To be a good asset to leverage, the mother ship has to be in great shape and, indeed, well looked after by trusted lieutenants to keep the home fires burning and fund/help new developments in the first instance.

Critically, a major influence on both the multiple and the ability to scale is impossible without, frankly, superb delegation; scaling up epitomizes divisions of labour and divesting workload. Even in technically driven companies, not everything can be automated and the human workforce becomes more important to ensure scalability and international growth.

The Assay approach illustrates exactly what inspired my initial research into delegation. Even if the goal is not to sell, but to increase the profitability and create a more resilient business, largely the same principles apply. Such activity requires strategic thought, which comes better from a clear mind. The plans that result need time to implement, time away from the day-to-day operation, which naturally become the focus areas on a Task List Profile as a management team decide what to delegate.

4
TYPES OF DELEGATION

'Delegation', as defined in the *Oxford English Dictionary*, is presented as a verb: 'to delegate', which is the act of entrusting a task or responsibility to another person, usually one more junior.

While this is of course correct, it doesn't really cover all that delegation is about. After all, one can delegate not just to a person but also to a process, system or, more spiritually, to a future point in time (let the universe decide!).

However, for our purposes, I identify and define four types of delegation: downward, with which we are most familiar and which is most closely aligned with the strict definition of the verb; upward, it happens in numerous ways and for numerous reasons but is the handing over of work from a subordinate to a superior; sideways, where work or responsibility is handed over to a teammate or from peer to peer; and silently, which is a definition out of context of the others but still a valid method of ensuring all types of delegation happen often unsuccessfully.

Downward delegation

This is the delegation type most of us are familiar with and have experienced either as a delegator or as a delegate. Naturally, when one transfers responsibility or delegates a specific task or tasks to someone who works for them (or over whom they have authority to delegate – either tacitly, verbally or contractually) it is generally 'downward' but the process remains the same for other types of delegation.

In a business sense, delegation in this way starts when an employee becomes a team leader or manager. Delegation is a skill but it is also a habit and thus very easy to dismiss as a management skill that is acquired early in the management journey and largely taken for granted throughout the manager's career. (See Chapter 13: Delegation as a new leader.)

Successful downward delegation happens when there is a clear understanding of what is required by all individuals to achieve the team's and/or organization's goals. Its priority, timing and importance as well as the expected standards and methods of its achievement are clear and agreed by all parties.

Poor downward delegation happens when there is a lack of any of the above, that is to say where what is required is misunderstood or there is not clarity on why this is required by the organization or the team or why this is required by the manager, or why this is required to be done by 'me' as a subordinate. Similarly, if its priority, timing and importance are not fully appreciated or the means of achieving it are neither recognized nor given to delegates, problems will arise.

Upward delegation

Poor downward delegation is the most likely cause of upward delegation. When upward delegation occurs and it is unwelcome, it is usually because something is amiss with the way work was delegated in the first place. Upward delegation is usually the task or update that hasn't been done and often the manager doesn't know it until it is a more urgent requirement that he or she then needs to pick up.

Upward delegation can happen when a subordinate finally admits far too late that for whatever reason this has not been done and some or all of the work needs to be carried out by the manager.

Upward delegation can also be far more subtle and almost unspoken. This is the scenario where the manager becomes afraid to delegate as a result of past attitude and response to delegation received from all or some of the team. Naturally, it could be construed as a simple barrier to delegation, and it is, but I also categorize it here as it is also a reverse delegation of sorts, where the subordinate *knows* that the manager is doing their work for them.

Upward delegation, however, can also be a good thing. If we literally take the meaning to be where a subordinate creates or hands back work to a manager then in the instance where a subordinate is proactively coming forward to request further knowledge, understanding, information or training on a particular issue or responsibility, upwards delegation is a good thing for the longer term. This creates a short-term increase in the manager's work as a direct result of the subordinate, but where it results in the ability of the manager to delegate more, it is a successful form of delegation which presents the opportunity for more successful downward delegation.

There is also a useful reference in Chapter 13 that highlights a case study rife with upward delegation.

In 'Where is the monkey?' by William Oncken and Donald L. Wass (1974, Harvard Business Review), tasks and workload are analogized to those of pet monkeys. The monkeys travel around on people's backs and require care and feeding by their owner. They can be transferred easily and are happy to go to anyone who promises to look after them.

The article begins with a scenario where a team member tells his manager of a problem, expecting the manager to use his limited knowledge to come up with a snap solution. Under pressure, the manager agrees to give it some thought. This is an example of upwards delegation and the monkey has now been transferred from the team member to the manager.

Even if the manager had deferred the delegation with a request for an email (leaving the next move to the team member), the onus would still be on the manager to reply. The monkey is ready to pounce from the subordinate's to the manager's back.

Add to this similar scenarios across the team and the manager becomes the bottleneck and the team become stuck and inhibited in their progress. He has a menagerie of monkeys.

The problem is that the responsibility is assumed right from the outset to be a joint one shared between manager and team member, that is the monkey straddles the back of both manager and team until it is clear who is going to look after it.

This situation has no good outcome. The manager is sinking under workload imposed upon him from above and below. His team regard him as a bottleneck who is poor at decision making and holding them back. The manager resolves to catch up over the weekend and turn over a new leaf from Monday.

Until he has an epiphany, brought on by the sight of his team enjoying a leisurely game of Saturday morning golf as he arrives at work. He recognizes that the more work he does, the more his team are likely to give him, and, frankly, why wouldn't they? He does a great job for them! This asks the question, 'Who is working for whom?'

His Monday is very different, each team member is invited into the office one by one and the team members are reminded that the monkeys are theirs to nurture and that the manager is there to help them with their monkey, not to adopt or foster it. The team members are invited to come and discuss their monkeys by appointment so that the manager can control the timing and content of the time in his diary.

My favourite line in this article really sums everything up. In the Monday meeting the manager says, 'At no time while I am helping you with this or any other problem will your problem become my problem. The instant your problem becomes my problem, you no longer have a problem. I cannot help a person who hasn't got a problem.'

The conclusion is all about managerial control of managerial time and refers liberally to the care and feeding of monkeys in a further analogy. In short, monkeys are fed – by appointment only and face to face or via telephone only (as opposed to email or documentation, which would require the manager to take action). Alternatively, they should be shot. Their population should be kept under control and their feeding times scheduled according to initiative. This latter point relates to the Check, Check, Report part of the delegation process discussed in this book, where the degree of initiative given to the team member determines the regularity and direction of reporting.

My second favourite line in this article is the last: 'All these steps [i.e. to manage the monkeys as per the above] will increase the manager's leverage and enable the value of each hour spent in managing management time to multiply *without theoretical limit*.'

Enough said.

Sideways delegation

There are numerous contexts for sideways or peer-to-peer delegation but in the main there are three: manager-to-manager delegation cross-functionally or cross-departmentally, where one manager picks up work ostensibly held from an accountability

perspective in the other's remit; teammate-to-teammate delegation, where tasks or responsibilities listed on one employee's job
description are handed over to another (whether the other's job
description includes the said tasks and responsibilities or not);
and inter-company delegation, which in the context of both
SMEs and corporations (of all denominations and charities) can
be classed as collaboration or joint ventures and outsourcing.

Sideways delegation has all the hallmarks, barriers and road
bumps as any other type of delegation. Where it happens well,
it results in all the same benefits and value of downward delegation. Where it works well, it results in a collaborative venture
that plays to the strengths of each party.

Where it happens less successfully, sideways delegation is
viewed within organizations as carrying a team member or
department function and in an inter-company relationship is a
poor client/supplier relationship.

Figure 4.1 illustrates these three types of delegation.

We can then expand this to illustrate how delegation is far from
downward only and how in fact it expands within and outside
the business to form a delegation stakeholder map. It's surprisingly far-reaching: Figure 4.2 is a delegation stakeholder diagram for a sole-trader website designer and Figure 4.3 for a
chain of international coffee shops.

Any stakeholder map is very much crystalized as the process of
delegation becomes clear. Note how similar the maps in Figure
4.2 and Figure 4.3 essentially are: delegation can be subsumed in

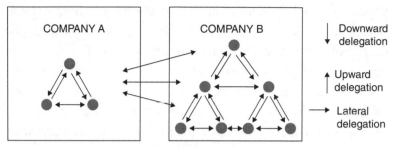

Lateral delegation within an organisation flows from peer-to-peer
Delegation which flows between companies is outsourcing
or collaboration

Figure 4.1   Types of delegation.

other key management, communication, social and relationship
skills. Any passing of any responsibility to another is essentially
delegation, and so to understand its place in the grander scheme
of things is essential if it is to work well.

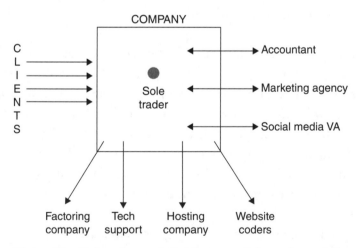

Figure 4.2   Delegation stakeholder map: Sole trader website
designer.

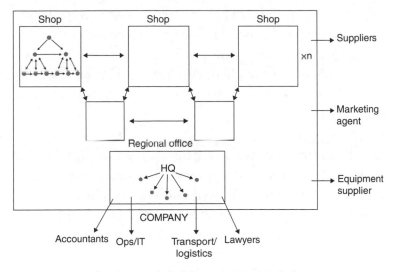

Figure 4.3   Delegation stakeholder map: National chain.

As the understanding deepens then one sees that many business interactions are actually acts of delegation. These maps show that both businesses have suppliers, to whom they effectively delegate some of their required business tasks and operations, and they also have clients who are effectively delegating to them in the same way.

So to understand delegation more fully and to get into the habit of delegation is to also recognize the opportunity to improve supplier relationships and deliver superior customer service.

Silent delegation

This is the delegation that happens between parties when nothing is said by way of a brief or request or work to be carried out. Silent delegation happens where a task or responsibility becomes apparent but is not instantly assigned to any particular person, team or department, usually because there is a lack of clarity about where it might or even should sit. A representative then volunteers to pick up that task or sees it as their responsibility to action it.

As with all the other types of delegation we've covered, silent delegation has a way of being very successful as well as highly disastrous. Where it works well and is at its best is in a well-honed team – any team, be it at home or at work. Silent delegation becomes a production line of happenings which combine and conspire to smooth the journey – for everyone involved. It is easy, known and flows faster than those interactions which require pause for communication or discussion. It is both conscious – in that is it relevant, agreed, clear and beneficial – and subconscious – in that it appears to 'just happen', for all the same reasons.

Where silent delegation is less successful and even has the potential to be disastrous is where tasks appear in an environment where relationships and remits are less clear. It is most easy to illustrate this point with an example. Imagine a meeting between managers in an organization, a task becomes apparent and it is not instantly clear where it should sit as a responsibility and therefore who – if anyone – in the room should pick it up. For whatever reason, the task becomes loosely assigned or even self-assigned to a member of the meeting, and because the discussion is fast moving and the task is quickly dealt with the meeting moves on. It may be that the best person or correct area now has the right task for them, but often this is not the case.

The task falls to the wrong person for any one of a number of reasons:

- Can't resist filling a gap.

- Can't say no.

- Feels obliged as a junior to put hand up.

- Overenthusiasm (wanting to impress).

In all instances, such responsibilities rarely go properly through the process of delegation, either there has to be an innate ability to fill in the process gaps (in which case the manager must be empowered to do so) or else time has to be made available after the meeting to make the task pre-SMART and SMART (both of which we will come on to in later chapters). Fundamentally, silence can be classed as a type of delegation, but it is a sophisticated one that requires a deeper understanding between parties (whether organizational, departmental or individual), though it often happens in environments or circumstances where this is not the case. This is the reason why it can be disastrous.

Where any delegation goes wrong, it can end up with any number of consequences for the organization, business or team, but usually, in the first instance, it results in upward delegation, or to refer to my favourite article on the subject, it results with the monkey being transferred back to the manager's back.[1]

---

[1] This article is 'Management Time: Who's got the monkey?' by William Oncken Jr. and Donald L. Wass and debuted in *Harvard Business Review* in 1974 (Nov/Dec).

Silent delegation and gender

Controversially, and anecdotally, I have noticed a link between silent delegation and gender. Generalization is necessary here but only to get the point across. Women, often more so as they mature and become mothers, appear to be more disposed to self-appoint or pick up tasks and work. They are often worse at being able to say no and are capable for this reason of biting off more than they can chew.

Men are also guilty of the same, of course, but less so and less for the people-pleasing motivations to which women are prone. If men pick up inappropriate tasks, it is more to do with ego and proof of ability than a desire to please.

Regardless, the consequences of poor silent delegation are the same for the outward stakeholder and can result in burnout, stress and loss of confidence for the individual(s) involved.

Stakeholders and the impact of business types on delegation

Whether or not we focus on delegation here or just on business complexity – and it follows that the more complex a business, the more complex the delegation process and interdependence is – the definition of delegation is deeper in a more complicated business.

The grid in Figure 4.4 was drawn up to illustrate to my own business partners the difficulty, but also the inherent value, of getting delegation right when it comes to business exit and ease of operation.

	Business involves				Example
	Technology	People	Service	Products	
					B2B supply and delivery
					TV channel
Level of business complexity increases					Golf club/hotel
					Consultancy/training
					Traditional retail
					Online functional and transactional site
					Online service delivery with online help/education
					Basic online retail

Figure 4.4 Business types.

Where the level of business complexity increases so does the aspect of the valuation multiple related to the reduction of dependence on the founders or the group who wishes to exit or sell.

Outside of a business valuation context, I also think the people involved in managing, running and developing the more complex businesses are the ones who should be remunerated most highly, but this is blatantly often not the case.

Back to stakeholders and the complexity of delegation, it is clear to see how deep delegation needs to go when a business involves people and service in its delivery. Add in technology (which is why we debate the very definition of delegation in the first place), and the fact that technical delivery requires service from people, and the scale and depth of delegation required to make it all happen successfully becomes clear.

The Gift of Time is accompanied by an online programme that offers practical help, activities and accountability for action.[2]

---

[2] For more information go to http://giftoftime.yourgoalstoday.com/.

Part Two
GETTING DELEGATION TO WORK

5
BARRIERS TO DELEGATION

If we look again and remind ourselves of the value and benefits of delegation, as I've illustrated them in this book, then delegating, that is to say delegating and delegating well, appears to be a no-brainer. Nonetheless, just like anything that has such wide-ranging advantages, it rarely comes easily, and the greatest reasons that stop it happening well (or even at all) are barriers which first need to be understood in order to be overcome.

Many of the managers and business owners I speak to about delegation highlight barriers to it and many refer to themselves as 'control freaks', that is as being unable or unwilling to let go or share their responsibilities with anyone. And yet, even before I started researching delegation in earnest, I knew instinctively that there was more to it than this, because ultimately there are very few people (i.e. nix) whom I have met who wouldn't value more time, or less work to do, and so even if they were worried about letting go many would be happy to do so because of the rewards (time/less work) on offer.

In the initial round of research the results were clear: time is actually and proportionately the biggest barrier to delegation. Often when I stand at the beginning of a workshop or in a keynote and ask for a show of hands, control or trust is identified as the likely biggest barrier in the room, but at the end it is generally agreed that – ironically and in the same way that money begets money – time is the biggest stopper to gaining more time.

Here's an extract from a blog I wrote entitled 'Money begets money and time begets time':

When I stand at the top of a workshop or keynote and ask who would like to have more time, there is usually a 100% show of hands. If delegation frees up time then surely it is a must? Everyone nods agreement, so when asked, what stops you delegating? It is usually 'control' that yields the greatest response on the first pass. By the end, time is usually the thing that everyone is looking to find in order to increase the delegation in their lives, jobs and businesses.

My own research shows the barriers – in order – to be:

Time

Trust/control

Money

Know-how

To really paraphrase, let's start at the bottom.

If you don't delegate enough because you don't know how, time in the first instance is likely to be what stops you from learning.

If you don't delegate enough because you don't have the money to outsource or employ anyone to help, more time would help you earn more in order to generate cash to pay someone else.

If you don't delegate enough because you don't trust anyone else to take on some of your workload or responsibilities, it is likely to be because you haven't taken the time to find a person you can trust and train them to help in a way that meets your timescales and standards.

And so if everything loops back to time, having time would enable one to create more time. Ergo, as the saying goes: money begets money, so time begets time. If we take each barrier in turn and examine it more closely, the link back to time becomes all the more evident.

Know-how

If you don't delegate enough because you don't *know how*, time in the first instance is likely to be what stops you from learning. My own research shows that 80% of managers are not actually sure how to delegate. I find this amazing on one hand, but logical on the other. It's tricky. Some of this inability (to delegate) comes from lack of confidence in their own position and sense of achievement, or lack of comfort with their own authority. In a corporate sense, in truth this is not how this should work at all and its roots, I think, lie in our shift away from older managers. The old way was years of experience (and limited reference to genuine evidence of leadership skills).

I've included a chapter in this book about leadership and new managers because it is incredible how many new managers without delegation training or experience turn into established or 'experienced' managers. This happens because of the marvel of inheritance, where everyone knows their job within the team and the manager doesn't actually ever have to delegate anything on their own initiative because it is already done and accepted by the team. It's therefore not surprising that know-how comes up a lot even from apparently established managerial or supervisory staff.

In an SME context, know-how is a biggie because 74.3% of the sector does not employ anyone but the business owner and the majority of the rest never will.[1] If they did, it would be under duress and, even if it were voluntary, their knowledge would be limited. Increasingly so, the act of being self-employed (see my blogs on zero hours contracts *et al.*[2]) is the act of creating your own small business but with no expectation of ever being any more than the only employee and therefore a means to creating one's own job. This means that the Office of National Statistics will no doubt find in the future that the number of SMEs employing anyone (currently only 25.7%) will drop even

---

[1] https://www.gov.uk/government/statistics/bis-business-population-estimates, accessed 10th October 2014.
[2] http://thegiftoftime.yourgoalstoday.com.

lower. A new category may or may not emerge in terms of self-employed categorization.

Knowing how to delegate for small business owners is essential even if they employ no one. It's common for small businesses to start their delegation journey with a bit of outsourcing to other companies, bookkeepers, virtual assistants, designers and so on. The principle of successful delegation remains the same and so therefore does the know-how, which is essential to get the best from the relevant suppliers. However, it's usually easier in a client/supplier relationship because the recipients of delegated work in this instance know their job and what is needed from their clients (or employers) and are expert at extracting this. The same is less true, of course, of employees and they are more likely to be much more dependent on the employer delegating well.

Know-how or lack of it covers a broad spectrum, and in research can come from simply not knowing how to start the process of recruiting or handing over, or from not knowing what to divest, who to look to for help and how to find them as well as knowing why it would be beneficial in the first place. We tackle all of this in later chapters of this book and through the associated online programme as an ongoing piece of learning.[3]

---

[3] *The Gift of Time* online programme that accompanies this book takes you through the process of delegation – from 'why' to 'how' – and includes activities and exercises that can be applied real time in the workplace or business. The programme can be long term and encourages full accountability for agreed actions.

In many leadership theories, I find delegation is regarded as a lowly one on the spectrum of management skills. Here I cite in particular a model from one of my MBA textbooks where delegation is clearly shown as a habit acquired early on in the journey of management development on a spectrum of increasingly masterful skills.[4] Kolb *et al.* portray delegation as being one of the lowliest of skills managerial toolset whereby entrepreneurialism is the apparent jewel in the glittering crown of successful leadership. I don't mean to sound disparaging but this theory backs up my own thought that delegation is somehow expected to come naturally; it's just a thing that managers acquire pretty early on in their career, almost through a process of osmosis. To my mind, it is comparable to parenting: just because we've all been children doesn't necessarily mean we'll all make good parents. More encouragingly, a research piece by Banford *et al.* has a reference point that is quoted as follows: 'Delegation is an under-researched management practice. This paper contributes to the delegation literature by exploring its value to management in a global context.'[5]

Money

In a small business, if you don't delegate enough because you don't have the money to outsource or employ anyone to help,

---

[4] Kolb, D., Lublin, S. Spoth, J. and Baker, R. (1986) 'Strategic Management Development: Using experiential learning theory to assess and develop managerial competencies, *Journal of Management Development*, 5(3): 13–24.

[5] C. G. Banford, C. G., Ronald Buckley, M. and Roberts, F. (2014) 'Delegation revisited: How delegation can benefit globally-minded managers', *International Journal of Physical Distribution & Logistics Management*, 44(8/9): 646–54.

more time would help you to earn more cash to pay someone else. The converse is therefore (as with needing time to get time) that you need money to get more money. In a large or small business it is simply a fact that you may not have the team members to delegate to or the finance to outsource work. Money is an issue, of course, but it can be overcome.

The origins of my research into delegation were driven by its potential economic and commercial value and so, in truth, money is therefore arguably one of the easiest to combat as a barrier. This is so for a number of reasons.

In challenging the traditional definition of delegation we open up the possibility of technology helping to facilitate delegation, especially if it is appropriate to start small with the easiest tasks. It is not appropriate to be specific here but safe to say that applications are available for next to no investment and are geared up to helping people streamline, offload or automate their workload. The point of this within the context of this book is that, in starting to delegate, people that I have worked with are encouraged to start small with basic elements of their workload and to enjoy the little benefits that this brings. It is also a micro trip through the delegation pathway, with all the same principles concerning time investment, thinking through processes, taking time to find the right application (as opposed to the right person), deciding on quality measures, checks and timescales. For next to no money, the delegation process can begin, and then be valued.

So, in most cases where money is the sticking point, the requirement is to build the case for delegation and the resources

THE GIFT OF TIME

required to action it. This is relatively easy in the context of an SME but regardless of your own vantage point (business owner or otherwise), to understand this section is a useful basis for building a case for recruitment or outsourcing in any context, either corporate or domestic.

Later on, we cover what to delegate and who to delegate to, but for now let's assume all of that has been done, or at least has been assessed through the completion of a Task List Profile and skillset identification (which we'll cover later in the book as part of your Delegation Plan). As part of this process, let's assume our case is a small business owner. It may or may not be a sole trader; it doesn't really matter at this point. The fact is it/he or she has decided to delegate and gone through a process of deciding what and to whom. It has costed this delegation, either through researching or deciding upon a fair market salary or through having its requirements estimated by a suitable supplier.

So in sparse terms, the owner knows how much the delegation is going to cost. Naturally, there is also the cost and opportunity cost of sourcing or recruiting the supplier or employee as well as time spent training and the lack of return that the employee brings until they are properly up to speed. Insofar as it can be estimated, all of these costs are ideally included in the business case to give a true reflection of the necessary investment and therefore a more accurate prediction of return.

Having fully documented the cost of delegation, it becomes time to return to the 'why'. Time and again, the 'why' (as in, 'Why do I want to delegate, what's in it for me?') question comes up. If you get a personal benefit or benefits from a certain action, the action itself becomes habit forming. This is why it is vital to keep that in mind, even if the result feels a long way off and always when things are not going right (we cover that later too).

In revisiting the 'why' at this point, it is with the intention of valuing it, or its potential. Table 5.1 lists some examples and how one might value their place in one's life.

I've always tried to find a way to delegate things I'm not keen on doing, or things I'm not good at. This, I think, has always been my natural default. However, when I set up my first ever business, I knew that its ability to grow and its value to any potential purchaser would be substantially higher the less dependent on me, or anyone else for that matter, it was. Even the very small business-for-sale agents acknowledge that a delegated business is worth twice as much.

Having valued the prospective benefits of the delegation, one is in a clear position to build a business case and/or return on investment, or ROI. For a business owner working as a sole trader, government statistics tell us that their average turnover will be £60k. If they plan to delegate 10% of even their 40-hour week, that's four hours. The work is basic admin and will cost them £20 per hour all told, so £80 per week. Their revenue per week based on their having no holiday at all during the year or, at least, continued income while they're away (note all of this serves to under-egg the financial benefit) is £1154. If they aim and manage to increase that by 20%, they will add £231 per week to their revenue, which works out as an 89% ROI. This is illustrated in Figure 5.1.

Table 5.1 Motivation to delegate.

What to do with the time gained back – 'why'	How to value it
Grow existing business or develop new products and services	How much by? Percentage of turnover, average value or profit of new sales/new clients × number gained over and above the expected or current level within a specified timescale.
Take time off	Naturally taking time off can be for a number of reasons and there isn't necessarily a financial measure for this. In this instance, think instead of the (if possible) financial implications of not taking the time off – which may therefore fall into other categories listed here.
Further career/find or develop a new role	As an employee, delegation is vital in order to further career. An employee who is renowned for being head down and hard at graft can be perceived as great by the employer and better for the business but the downside is that the employee – who is often a source of a wealth of information about the business, its processes, culture and customers – doesn't have the time or opportunity to assist in the forward development of the business. As for themselves, employees who develop themselves and their own career path are looking for new challenges and the ability to add more value within or without their current employ and it is always better that they delegate and find new ways to assist those above them to in turn delegate to them and benefit the business accordingly.

(continued)

Table 5.1   *(continued)*

What to do with the time gained back – 'why'	How to value it
Pursue a hobby or exercise Spend time with family Recover from or prevent illness	When we move to benefits that are related to time away from the work as a result of delegation for whatever reason it is useful to think of the drawbacks of not doing it.
Start or buy a new business	The logic here follows that of business growth, to add to personal wealth or one's desired financial target through starting something new. The estimated outcome of starting something new is a clear way of valuing delegation potential and the promise of that achievement may be the motivation required to clear the way.

Thus in regarding delegation and in particular its costs as an investment, we can treat such investment with the expectation of a return and, in doing so, build a business case for delegating in the first place.

Of course, the above is an extremely simple example but it works for everyone if they can find a way to value the benefit. In this example, if the uplift had been only 7% the costs would still have been covered. Health, happiness, the opportunity to retire can be argued as priceless and therefore very difficult to value, especially in advance when the risk is there that

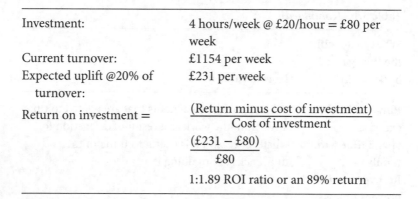

Investment:	4 hours/week @ £20/hour = £80 per week
Current turnover:	£1154 per week
Expected uplift @20% of turnover:	£231 per week
Return on investment =	$\dfrac{\text{(Return minus cost of investment)}}{\text{Cost of investment}}$
	$\dfrac{(£231 - £80)}{£80}$
	1:1.89 ROI ratio or an 89% return

Figure 5.1 Delegation and return on investment.

it doesn't happen, but for sure if nothing changes, nothing will change.

For an employee, if you're not directly involved in sales or represent more of a cost centre, it's clearly more tricky. There is, however, always a way, because delegation done right (in the right way, of the right things, to the right person and for the right reasons) simply always has benefits that can be valued.

Here's a lovely example from a firm whose 'heads of' are involved in a session thinking about delegation and gaining financial benefits in order to build their case for getting more staff. The timing is in the midst of our recent hard-bitten recession and they're feeling overworked, underpaid and distinctly overqualified for a lot of what they are being asked to do. During the part where they are asked to identify – through a Task List Profile – what they would and should most like to delegate, the head of HR talks about reviews that she has to do, write up and add to staff records on a central database.

The meetings themselves, she likes; typing up the notes of the meeting, she deplores; and she is not great at the online filing of things either. It drains her energy. She has to gear herself up to do the latter parts and often ends up late with them as they just do not feel like a priority. She has no one to delegate to, particularly because any staff member would need to be in the HR department to protect staff privacy and there is not the budget to provide her with anyone. She could definitely outsource the typing but knows that when other 'heads of' are also screaming for resources she is unlikely to get authority for the budget.

As she describes her situation, the head of IT starts to fidget. He wants to say something and can't wait until she finishes. He has an idea and asks if the meeting would be okay to be recorded. She replies that providing the staff member was aware and the recording was kept private she saw no reason why not. He beams and suggests that she could therefore use a software program used elsewhere in the business to record and upload the meeting to the same staff record ready to be searched and listened to if required. A deal is done (sideways or peer-to-peer delegation, which plays to strengths) and he agrees to set it up forthwith. It doesn't take her long to start doing the maths and recognize that in saving the proportion of her salary devoted to doing reviews three times a week she has built a case for delegation. She knows exactly what she wants to do with the six hours a week minimum she has just saved and knows therefore what her next project is going to be and how to value the resources needed.

For the sake of pedantry (and in order for me to claim a victory for delegation), this is the assumed value of that little transaction:

Head of HR annual salary	*£70 000*
Pay per week (excluding employer costs)	*£1346*
Pay per hour @ 37.5 hours per week	*£36*
Number of reviews per week	*3*
Time typing up/uploading per review	*2 hours*
Time saved per week	*6 hours*
Financial 'saving' per annum	*£11 000 plus*

By saving it is appreciated that the salary will still be paid to the Head of HR but it then becomes what she does with that time – to develop her role, department, career – that is of distinct benefit and similarly able to be valued financially at a later point in terms of its benefit. Therefore in this case, the delegation potential is worth so much more than the £11 000 calculated above. So if money is the issue stopping delegation then the answer to overcome it is to regard it as an investment, play it safe, start small and see the return. Taking the time to do this, rather than rest on gut feel, is essential, because if money is spent and delegation doesn't go well, the effect is double reverse. The spending stops, the work is clawed back and the symptoms and frustrations of less delegation rear their ugly head again.

Trust/control

If you don't delegate enough because you don't trust anyone else to take on some of your workload or responsibilities, it is likely to be because you haven't taken the time to find a person you can trust and train them to help in a way that meets your timescales and standards. It's also quite possible that you don't have the money to take the time or the know-how that tells you how much sense it would make to invest the money and time. I'm aware I'm tying up my own barrier definitions here and blurring the lines to confuse. I do that deliberately to illustrate that all barriers are relevant depending on the journey; at times, some or one will be more prevalent than others and that will be a fairly moveable feast.

It's not that I don't trust anyone ... it's just that I am a control freak.

It's necessary for me to club trust and control together as I see them as the same thing. I appreciate that I am often alone in this view. My basis sits in the fact that I often hear words akin to 'I'm a control freak', 'I don't like to let go', 'I prefer to do it myself', 'I'm not sure anyone could do it like I do', 'I know my own business better than anyone else does', 'There are some things other people can't do' and so on. Guffaw, guffaw, I'm a control freak and that's a good thing. Being a control freak means one thing: you do not or cannot trust anyone else to do it for you. You are more likely to stay small as a business owner, restrict your skill set and experience as an employed manager and frankly break or burnout either way. I say that as a classic control freak myself.[6]

---

[6]This is entirely my own observation of myself and is therefore entirely unqualified, but I often wonder whether some of my more disastrous delegation has happened because I have banished my control freakery into the realms of dispassion in order to be able to 'let go and forget about it' rather than embracing it as a basis for great delegation because I have exacting standards and clarity on what is an acceptable level of performance.

And if we get to that then as a client you are manna from heaven, because control freaks, or those who are prone not to trust others, are often the absolute best delegators in my observation (of hundreds of people). Here is an extract from a blog I wrote in 2012:

By their own admission, control freaks find it hard to let go, hard to believe that someone else will do as good a job, believe that only they can uphold their own standards and are reluctant to release time to hand over workload to someone else.

So why on earth might they make the best delegators? Delegation is an art form and it takes some doing. Those who do it well – like anything – get the most out of it and whilst control freaks take the most persuading to hand over elements of their business, they do it with thought and precision, clear briefing and clear expectation. They almost never just dump and run.

In addition, when it comes to using a call answering service or a virtual assistant (or Virtual PA Company for both), those who take the time to consider their requirements and expectations and bother to bash out and agree a process for each scenario (assuming your provider is receptive to this) get far better service.

My point is that once that trust issue is overcome, usually because a good job is being done and the delegator feels able to hand over more and check up less, the ability to let go of more grows. The delegator gets time to develop the business or the career and the benefits defined in the original 'why' become all the more real and achievable.

Naturally, though, if the trust turns out to be misplaced, for whatever reason, the work is not done well or in a timely manner or the delegate is just not performing, the delegator feels justified in his or her original belief that delegation was a bad thing because no one else can do it as well. Work is taken back, the delegator believes the 'why' to be unachievable and the status quo resumes (I refer the reader to Chapter 6: Over-capability.)

And here it is, the loop back to time. To overcome the fear of losing control when delegating one has to take *time* to think about what would be best to delegate – to start with, what the recipient would need to know in terms of timescales, standards, processes, systems and feedback in order to make it a more comfortable arrangement. Time to find the right person qualified to perform the tasks, right, in terms of chemistry and cultural fit, to stand a chance of making it work; and time to coach and mentor them, as well as train them to execute the work, hopefully without stifling any natural creativity and input that the incoming delegate may have to contribute.

Back to time

Given that time is the biggest output and also benefit to delegation, it also figures that time is the biggest barrier and time is the method to getting over that barrier.

A business partner of mine is always saying that sometimes you have to slow down to speed up. This is the case with delegation. You reach a point that, whatever your personal barrier is – know-how, trust/control or money – you have to take time to overcome it. Time to learn, time to recruit/train/manage, time to build the case for investment as well as, in all cases, time to think about what to delegate, time to think about when to delegate, who to delegate to and how to delegate and manage the recipient of delegated work.

So if investing money hopefully means that more money results, so investing time hopefully means that more time results. What one does with the resulting time is the ultimate benefit of delegation.

6
OVER-CAPABILITY

The definition of 'over-capability' here is mine. There will be someone else's, I'm sure, but as I can't find it defined as a single, albeit hyphenated, word you'll just have to bear with my interpretation for the purpose of getting through this chapter:

Over-capability – the ability to capably turn one's hand to just about anything and do it to at least an acceptable standard...

...and then get trapped into doing it all the time, either by one's own or others' expectation.

I see this skill – blight? misfortune? – in many people, probably in my case because of the work I do, but most probably, not exclusively per se, and in particular in entrepreneurs (and, interestingly, mothers too).

So have you ever been called or thought of yourself as a jack of all trades yet a master of none? Business owners can be a classic example of over-capability, of losing their focus to a multi-disciplined career in which they fail to excel. They start either as a one-man band or usually as a small team that is called upon to at least think about, if not execute, tasks and skills that are not necessarily its forte. As a business owner, or let's say entrepreneur, it is almost essential to be able to cover ground of all the major disciplines: sales, marketing, new product development, operations, finance and IT. Moreover, these people often find it easy to turn their hand to just about anything and manage not a half-bad job of it.

But there has to be a balance ... and just because you can doesn't mean you should. Fabulous to have a great grasp on what goes on in the business and how it gets done, but making the shift from 'doing' to 'getting it done' is an important part of the delegation process as well as a growth mindset.

Heard this one? If you want something done, ask a busy person. I agree with it, it's true and over-capable people usually have a problem with saying no (see Chapter 4's section on silent delegation) and taking it on themselves. People with a delegation mindset don't take on the monkey but they help with the monkey and facilitate the monkey-handler to do it or get someone else to help.[1]

Over-capability is a business, career and relationship breaker. If an entrepreneur gets too caught up in the minutiae – because he or she can and understands them so well, possibly better than

[1] W. Oncken Jr. and D. L. Wass (1974) 'Management Time: Who's got the monkey?' *Harvard Business Review*.

anyone else involved in the business – growth and stability suffer. If a manager does the same, they are at risk of breaking, risk of boredom, risk of being passed over and at risk of their own team leaving them because there is potentially limited empowerment. Someone above you who takes every opportunity to let you know that they know as much if not more than you do is intimidating. Someone who you can go to when you get stuck is a massive support.

I am still guilty of over-capability. In the first business I set up, I made the mistake of being over-capable, and I very much have to manage my relationship with that business even today because I can so easily slip into being so capable that instead of remembering that I set up the business to serve me, I become a servant to it (the nemesis of the delegation principle). Contrast this with the case study of Gems Lingerie, singularly the easiest business I have ever set up because it had to fit around me and primarily because I knew nothing about fashion design, fabrics, sewing, manufacturing or online marketing and was forced to defer to experts. The irony is, my ability to become partner in some seven businesses – Richard Branson, I am only 293 behind you! – was because of a renewed determination to delegate well, to the right people, with the right skills, better than mine, because I had learnt to accept that the right people may actually be better than me. While there is a need for me to understand (and manage) their role, there is less need for me to feel a sense of competition when it comes to allowing them to do the best they can do or for me to feel inferior because I do not understand it to the nth degree.

7
THE DELEGATION MINDSET

The shift from a 'do' to a 'get done' mentality is a big one and an essential part of becoming a delegator. Staying in the get done, rather than the do, mindset is a habit as well as a skill. Reverting to a 'doing' frame of mind means that one sinks into the detail of sweating the small stuff, head down, hard at work. Being responsible for getting things done, is different: it means facilitating others to do the work through recruitment, selection, training, coaching, follow up and feedback.

There are many analogies I could slip in here: conductor of an orchestra, ballet teacher, football manager, baseball coach. They all have one thing in common: they are not in the limelight, their team does the work that gets noticed, they may get shared credit for the results but they don't (visibly) play an instrument, pirouette, kick a ball or make a run, but they do help to make it all happen.

The mindset of a delegator keeps this in mind and stays off the pitch. It's the only way they can see the whole game. But without getting all lofty about it, delegation is not about dumping or abdicating responsibility; knowing what team members do and go through to achieve it is important. It's the way that improvements and change happen. Striking the balance is an interesting debate and I have no answer because I believe at any point the most senior manager can be thrown back into the thick of it when required. Maintaining the helicopter/bigger picture or strategic view, however, is what differentiates them from the team around them.

And this takes time, effort, energy, respect and understanding and, I think, a dose of humility. I'm often thrown back into the arguably 'more junior' roles that exist in my businesses. I've done my fair share of serving in shops, pricing products and services, handling calls, sorting out IT issues, sourcing (well, all kinds of stuff), setting up processes, sending emails, setting up spreadsheets or whatever. The fact is that it is a team effort and it is also important to at least have an understanding of the principles of what is required if one is intending to manage, give feedback on or critique the work of another. I don't have an answer on how deep this knowledge should go as a blanket response because it varies according to the roles, responsibilities and requirements of a given business or organization. Naturally, in some instances one recruits others for their expertise and so cannot 'do' their job per se, but as a manager they need to be able to manage to ensure the work gets done.

We all, as delegators, will find our level, but I love this role, which – to be honest – I only found existed very recently, that of a 'swing' in a theatre production. I quote here with kind courtesy of a website called playbill.com and Wikipedia.

Swing, a term in musical theatre for an understudy who prepares several roles.

Wikipedia

'Swings' are vital positions in the cast of a Broadway musical. They need to be able to step into any one of a number of roles at a moment's notice. You can only imagine the amount of hard work and dedication it takes to prepare for a role on Broadway. Now multiply that by, say, a *dozen* roles and you get an idea of what it's like to be a swing.

Consider it an understudy of sorts. A swing's role is to fill in for a member of the ensemble when he or she is out of a show.

Playbill.com

In a sense of reverse delegation, this is a role that is both 'superior' and 'inferior' in the traditional or managerial sense. Inferior in that the swing picks up other roles that others can't do but superior in that they have a very wing-side role and ability to see the contribution that everyone makes to the whole show. Great delegators can still find themselves in this position, capable of doing every role in the team but staying offstage nonetheless. Their potential weakness is their strength, their ability and therefore the temptation to step in, take over and micro manage as a result of the blessing of their knowledge.

Contrast this with the role of a film director, often not trained to be an actor (or indeed any other role within film production) and one sees a different approach to 'delegation'. The director cannot or at least is unlikely to pick up an acting role – or any other. In fact, in the words of one director worthy of any acting role (Richard Attenborough) as quoted by another class act (Anthony Hopkins) and somewhat paraphrased here, 'You are the actor and I trust you to do that as that is the contract you have signed, but if you can't do it, then it has to be goodbye.'

My point is that, however one arrives at it, from whatever background or experience, the delegation mindset is common regardless; it is one of allowing and facilitating others to get the work done while retaining responsibility for their actions and appropriate credit for their performance.

Delegation and mistakes

If we agree that we learn from our mistakes then in delegating we need to accept that of others too. Ouch.

There are many one-liners and quotes out there about how it's okay to make mistakes and that's how we learn etc. It is very true, and, as already mentioned, the fear of things going wrong is also a barrier to delegation happening at all, let alone happening effectively. My favourite quote, though, comes from Rupert Everett on the BBC's *Andrew Marr* show, he said, 'Failure is the manure from which we grow.' I like that. In terms of delegation, it means we have to expect and allow that those to whom we delegate at times will make mistakes, as we will, and we have to be ready not only to react to those errors, sub-standards and seconds going out (if not in our name then at least under our brand) and to be supportive, constructive and progressive in dealing with them and the circumstances that result.

This also affects deciding why, what, who and how one delegates. It means that one has to consider what could go wrong (possibly by virtue of history and experience), what one might put in place to mitigate the possibility and the consequences of mistakes that do slip through and the actions required as a result. This is all part of the time that delegation takes, because none of this can happen and be perfect overnight, and it is also why time remains the biggest barrier to delegation.

The Gift of Time is accompanied by an online programme that offers practical help, activities and accountability for action.[1]

---

[1] For more information go to http://giftoftime.yourgoalstoday.com/.

Part Three
YOUR DELEGATION PLAN

8
STEP 1: WHY DELEGATE?

I n my research on delegation, and in the books that I've read
and the blogs, comments and bits I've read on the internet, as
well as the knowledge I've gained around business people of all
shapes, sizes and persuasions, the story rarely starts with 'why'.
Usually anything on delegation starts with 'how'.

I'll dwell on this a little as I believe it is important and, moreover, in the 'why' lies the crux of the motivation to get it right. If
we dive straight into thinking about how, or who, we are more
likely to be delegating because we can or because we ought and
less because we have thought through the true benefits: to us as
delegating individuals, to them as individuals being delegated
to, to it as an entity (be it a business, team, family, department
or organization).

In our delegation plan, we start with 'why', and cover 'what' and
'who' *after* we tackle the 'why'. I find this as a process much more
effective in establishing the delegation habit and forming clarity

on its benefits directly to the individual, which in turn cements and promulgates the habit itself.

So, at the outset, whether you are reviewing your delegation methodology, strategy or simply thinking about delegating for the first time, either to a new leader or as a business person, it is vital you start with the question 'Why?' Why, as in, 'What's in it for me?' even if it is growth for someone else. The reason for this is that we are programmed to be egocentric and so if you start with the benefits to you, and keep reminding yourself of what your delegation aims to achieve *for you* (even when it's hard work and even if or when it goes wrong) then you are more likely to stick with it and work to establish the habit.

Often when I work with clients, it is rare, even as a one-man band, that they delegate nothing at all. More often, anyone I work with delegates something. In employment, even those who are yet to manage a team of their own delegate their IT to the IT department if they think about it laterally enough. The self-employed rarely do their own accounts, for example, and even if they run their own accounting business and they do everything, they usually have or have had a cleaner or a gardener, or, if we have to push it, a builder, plumber or electrician because they understand the associated peace of mind and benefits of 'outsourcing' or, in practice, delegation. They do this because they instinctively – even if they don't think about it too much – understand the benefits such things bring; even if there is a price to pay for the plus side, the value outweighs it and the decision to delegate is made and so a habit starts to form.

The 'why' then, in truth, is a very personal thing – that's important. Having an ulterior motive is okay here. In fact, it is essential. It doesn't have to be complicated, nor does it have to be secret. As I say throughout this book, honesty and open communication are fundamental aspects of successful delegation. We all need to know *why* and we all need to know *why should I* – as in 'Why should I delegate?' and 'Why should I receive this delegation/delegated responsibility?' – and if the benefits to all parties involved are clear (NB. the more personal the better here) then the more successful the process of delegation is likely to be.

It may also be helpful at this juncture to form a case for 'why not', as in 'Why not delegate?' In case it needs saying out loud: what are the consequences of not delegating? So if you ask yourself, 'Why am I not delegating, either at all or not enough?' then I can think of a number of arguments to hang onto your workload:

- You retain more control.

- You retain more ownership (of style, IP, profits).

- You are gainfully/fully employed.

- Much less and possibly nothing gets done when you are ill/away/on holiday.

- You get to do repetitive tasks.

- You remain confined by your own capacity.

You may have more to add. Likely phrases that ultimately end up meaning the same as the above are:

- 'I'm a control freak.'

- 'I like to make sure things are done my way.'

- 'No one else can do it like me.'

- 'I'm not prepared to take the risk of things going wrong or not getting done.'

- 'I might make myself redundant.'

- 'What would I do then?'

- 'My business is too little.'

- 'I can't afford it.'

- 'I've done it before and it didn't work.'

- 'You just can't get the staff!' or 'I'd never find anyone I could trust.'

A downside of playing the superman card, or endeavouring to do everything, is that if you're operating to capacity and a new opportunity or a problem comes up, you may have to pass on the former to accommodate the latter. (NB: This can happen even if you are a good delegator and prone to keeping busy – it happens to me as I am inclined to be very nosy and interested in picking up new projects.) This, however, is more a case of time management, when something comes up (even if at first it is a problem), I'm still largely choosing to deprioritize something I love doing for something else I love doing. When the proverbial matter hits the fan in the life of a poor delegator, he or she ends up giving up something they'd like to do for stuff they'd rather not take on.

Note I presented consequences and not advantages here. The top three can probably loosely be construed as advantages if that floats your boat; and if it does, good (though you're probably reading the wrong book). And anyway, how many times have you heard someone preferring to have a smaller portion of something larger?

Hopefully, then, aside from this, the preceding chapters have given sufficient food for thought, if not direct incentive to get on with delegating; if not, or you're just dipping in here, let's summarize.

There's value in delegation. I believe, and am living proof of the fact – that delegation frees up time and head space enough to enable strategic and creative thinking about how to generate growth and wealth in business. If you're a business owner then the wealth generated is yours; if you're employed then generating growth/or other cost-saving initiatives for the business is always a good thing; but more pertinently to the individual, if you delegate well as a manager then you are naturally more available to your colleagues and superiors and developing your own skill set and career prospects, which naturally adds to your personal worth, value and wealth.

There are other benefits which we've touched on in addition to value but, in short, more time leads to more choice, about everything, one chooses what one wants to do (because everything else can and actually should be delegated to someone more suited to that responsibility), one plays to one's strengths – which leads to a happier individual and all the residual benefits transferred to those around them. In addition, when stress or pressure is relieved, we all recognize the ability to 'think straight', or, as we said above, more strategically or creatively. We all recognize the need to look after ourselves, physically and mentally, and yet at times we are, especially if we're ambitious, inclined to disregard this fact and plough on regardless. This often less productive way of working then reduces our innate ability to perform well, and leads to the potential for repeated mistakes, lack of progress or generally knowing in our hearts that we are not performing to our best potential. Even if others don't so much notice, this still takes its toll on self-confidence, which often means we work harder, push ourselves too much and continue to perform less well as a consequence, thus forming a circle of decline and creating a negative feedback cycle. So to avoid this and look after ourselves properly, to have time to think about our life's direction at home and at work, we can't be overloaded – and to unload, one way or another, is to delegate. A great part of my personal 'why' – as well as adding value and growth to the businesses I am involved in – was to spend time with my children and look after my health. Feeling good is an essential part of performing well – at anything: parenthood, fitness and exercise, partnership as well as management, teamwork and business.

However, you get to your why: what do you want, what do you do best, what do you not like doing, what would you like to start, what would you like to grow, sell or see, my advice is to indulge yourself and enjoy the process of deciding what you're going to get out of delegation. The clearer you are about 'What's in it for me?', the more likely you are to be motivated to get it right.

Treat the process of deciding your 'why' like a bucket list or a lottery win, make a list or know it in your heart: how will you spend more time (and/or more money)?

Gems start-up case study: Part 1

My close friend Emma and I decided to start Gems Lingerie one day when we were out for a run. All the businesses I've ever started or been involved with have been related to a product or service that I personally buy into as a consumer, usually because I can't already get what I want, or get what I want to the standard or spec that I want it. Gems was no exception. Gems knickers accommodated all the emergency or unexpected leakages that women have to cope with throughout their life.

We were both in the market for such a product but we're both busy ladies with other things to do during the day. In truth, we weren't at the time really looking to start a business but the product need arose and the decision was made.

Delegation from the start was going to be important, and here's the 'why':

- We were busy and had limited time but also felt that the business had potential to be significant and that time was of the essence as small, because similar (but not quite so good) brands were starting to sprout up in the US and their spread into the UK was only a matter of time.

- We were not experts in design, manufacture or distribution of anything, let alone anything as specialist as lingerie, and so we needed to hand this over to others who were better than us at this.

- We needed to do this because it gave us stretch and we didn't want to be doing stuff we don't thoroughly enjoy.

- This business needed to scale, quickly. It was not a mom and pop kitchen tabletop business. It was serious and sophisticated. We needed scalability and credibility from day one.

- We were looking for a speedy lack of involvement in the business. We only wanted the fun stuff. In addition, we were looking to build value for exit (in case we ever decided to) by not having the business dependent on us operationally to run it.

Our measures for how well we were doing with this business would come from the following statements as facts:

- We're having fun.

- We can fit everything into the time we have available.

- We're relaxed and unpressured, even though progress is being made and deadlines are being met.

- We've a credible and fast-moving business.

- We're enjoying the people we're working with and are happy with their performance.

- We're making money from a resilient business that is attractive to potential purchasers.

Having clarity on the 'why' is essential in order to measure success, so while it sounds an obvious thing, unless you understand why you have embarked on delegation in the first place it is impossible to understand how you are doing and to get the positive feedback needed to keep going and achieve all that delegation can bring to you.

The interesting thing about the measures for success listed above is that they are as applicable to us as the people delegating as they are to those being delegated to.

By looking at all aspects of the design, manufacture and operation and delegating wherever possible, we play to everyone's strengths. Everyone gets to join in our 'success' list:

- They're having fun.

- They can fit everything in.

- They're relaxed and unpressured even though progress is being made and deadlines are being met.

- They're part of a credible and fast-moving business.

- They're enjoying the people they're working with and are happy with their performance.

- They're making money from a resilient business.

This case study is broken down across this book into the constituent parts that match the delegation pathway, so in the next instalment we will look at 'what' needed to be delegated to make the business happen and 'who' we needed to find accordingly.

9
STEP 2: WHAT TO DELEGATE?

Of all the parts of the delegation process, this is the one that I love most. When you have achieved successful delegation of your least favourite areas of responsibility and everything is getting done on time (or even faster than before) to a standard you can be proud of, there is no better feeling.

Deciding what to delegate may already be clear to you, and even if it is, the following process is a useful one to put yourself through at any point. I do it every time I take anyone through it myself and it always throws up something of use. My mission in life is to only do what only I can do, so I am very on the case with delegating as much as possible to the right people with the right clarity, training or briefing, standard and measures agreed up front. So what this exercise throws up for me mostly these days is how I can effect change for the better in my life and business by removing anything that sinks my energy and keeping with that which plays to my strengths and keeps my motivation and energy high.

Like any strategy, those supported by an organized plan are the ones most likely to succeed. So here's how to get clear on what you need to delegate and what you can delegate.

Small tasks loom large

Deciding 'what' to delegate can be difficult, which is why I recommend what I call a Task List Profile, but I don't want to get all 'processy' here. I'm keen to make a really easy quick fix point: if you're struggling to know where to start when it comes to delegation, bear in mind that small tasks loom large.

Little things can sometimes hold us back the most. Indeed, most people would agree that a full-scale disaster is usually made up of a number of fairly small (and usually cope-able-with) errors or problems that combine with devastating effect. To this end, tackling, or more appropriately getting rid of, those tiny little horrors that take up too much space in your mind and eat away at your ability to get on with what you're best at, enjoy most and will take greatest satisfaction from, is vital.

I call them 'shoulder-sinkers'. Shoulder-sinkers get shuffled, many times, before they actually get done. The definition of shuffling tasks, in my book, looks something like this:

Imagine that email in your inbox or letter/report/piece of paperwork in your in-tray that gets opened or picked up, glanced over, thought about for a split second (usually the thought goes along the lines of 'Must do that,' before you put it down or close it and vow to do it later. And even if that whole process only takes a few seconds each time, if you include the number of times you just *think* about its needing to be done and multiply that by however many emails you have in your inbox and pieces of unattended paper there are in your in-tray, you will find that you are spending a great deal of time and effort on *not* achieving many things.

These things are important to identify and jettison wherever possible. Here's a simple confession of my own. I am rubbish – rubbish! – at posting stuff. I have stamps in my purse at all times and a franking machine at the office, a great memory for addresses and postcodes and a not bad record to accompany it. However, for some reason, when it comes to going to the post box (and worse if it requires an actual trip to the post office) any semblance of organization when it comes to deadlines is lost to putting off the posting thing. Why? No idea, but I've always been the same. I will therefore, sadly, never be an eBay millionaire, but my track record with such stuff increased tremendously when I was able to delegate the job of posting to my children, who were more than happy to run across to the post office in return for a small treat or little financial incentive.

My other is form filling or creation: it's just not going to happen (quickly anyway) and I find it is always worth training someone up to do it instead. Whatever your shoulder-sinkers are, each one is probably something small that takes up a disproportionately large amount of your time that it would be well worth your while finding someone else to do them for you, especially if that someone was motivated by the type of work you wanted them to take on.

This is because tiny things niggle and take up space and time that they are simply not entitled to do, which distracts you from priorities and enjoying other things to the full. So if you're up for a bit of delegation, think first about the things that take the wind out of your sails and the smile off your face and find someone for whom they have the opposite effect (and they will be out there) to take them on. Good luck: I know it will make a big difference, if only to the progression of your frown lines!

Start with a list of all your areas of responsibility and then break them down into subgroups of tasks – the more you can break these down the better. I call it a Task List Profile (Figure 9.1).

Task List Profile

In the first column next to the tasks, go through the list, line by line and (honestly) rank each task in terms of its dependency on you. So if it's something that truly only you can do, rank it H for high. If it's something that someone else could do for you if they needed to be trained up accordingly and monitored for a period to ensure standards and timescales were being met, rank it M for medium. It follows that any task which could easily be done by someone else ranks L for low.

Task Profile

Guidelines
Please use the grid to list all the tasks you currently have to deal with during a given period (week, month, year – but make sure they're all there). They can be generic but the more specific the better.

Dependence grading
Once listed, please grade each task by its dependence on you, i.e. :

(H) = High. Highly dependent on you to be completed. A task that is difficult to delegate by virtue of your specialism or skill, not because it would take time to train someone to do it.

(M) = Medium. Dependent on you to a certain degree but could be delegated to the right resource with an investment of time on your behalf or training.

(L) = Low. Easy to delegate to the right resource (NB. whether you have the funds for additional resource is irrelevant; the principle is how easy it would be to give away if you did).

Please try not to stray into the territory of how much you enjoy a task at this point. Simply focus on how important it is that you do it and no one else.

Enjoyment grading
The second column is all about enjoyment, but please turn your attention to that after the first column is completed so as not to blur boundaries. Once again, please grade each task according to how much you enjoy it, assuming you have the time to do it properly without being rushed or feeling under pressure. Do this regardless of perceived skill or ability of other people to do it for, even if it's 'cakes for team meeting' or 'walking the office dog'.

(H) = High. This is you in your element. You love these tasks. They give you the biggest buzz and you find them highly motivational. You may find that these are ones that get left because there are other 'priorities' that take precedent.

(M) = Medium. Maybe for these you have to be in the mood or maybe you have to psyche yourself up a little for these, but you largely enjoy them in the end or at least once they're done. It may be that the process is laborious but the outcome is enjoyable.

(L) = Low. These tasks drain energy. They loom large but give no satisfaction. You may put them off (and so waste time in doing so). They make your shoulders sink at the thought but come under the category of 'necessary evil'.

Tip: When grading tasks in either column, if in doubt, DOWN GRADE.

Task listing	Dependence rating (H/M/L)	Enjoyment rating (H/M/L)	Timing	Who
Emails	M	L		Team
Booking rail tickets	L	L		Team
Car insurance	L	L		Team
MAS form filling	M	L		Partners
System research	H	M		Team
Staff recruitment	M	H		Manager
Website writing	H	H		
Book writing	H	H		
GT website	H	H		
GT social media for book	M	M		Outsourced
VPA social media	M	M		Outsourced
Financial model	H	H		
Month-end process	M	L		Team
Accounts	M	M		Team/outsourced
Sage entry and credit control	M	L		Team
VAT returns	M	L		Team
System development and migration	M	M		Part team
Mentoring/partnering	H	H		
Business conferences and events	H/M	H/M		Shared with manager
Networking	H/M	H/M		Shared with manager
Speaking	H	H		
Online course design	M	H		Partnered
Workshop design	M	H		Partnered
Workshop delivery	L	L		Partnered

Comments or observations:

Figure 9.1 The Delegation Programme Task List Profile.

It is important through this part of the process that you are not sidelined by the existence or not of someone to delegate to. It's important not to think of the resources or whether they are present or indeed affordable; the exercise is primarily to identify what could, in an ideal world, be delegated, unfettered by any barriers such as time (to think, train or recruit), money (to pay or lose by virtue of going through the process), trust (what you daren't let go of, even if you know you should) or know-how (how on earth to start handing everything over). I'm sharing my own Task List Profile (Figure 9.1), as it stood when I first started to research delegation in 2013. It's great to look back on for me, as absolutely everything on this list is now delegated apart from those highlighted and, though I periodically revisit my current Task List Profile, the truth of the matter is everything in the second column is marked H and so I've no need to go any further.

I've no doubt that at some point some shoulder-sinkers will creep in but they will not be permitted to stay for long.

Task List Profile second column

In the second column, after the tasks, honesty here is just as important. You now need to rank each task in terms of how much you enjoy that item. It doesn't matter how easy or difficult you find it, and don't be tempted into the 'Well I don't so much enjoy it, but it only takes a few minutes' trap. Such tasks have a nasty habit of building up, taking over and draining energy and – guess what? – not being done. If a task is one you adore and something you spring out of bed in the morning for, rank it H for high. If it's something you don't so much mind but it is not your *raison d'être*, mark it as M for medium or, obviously, L for those tasks that are low on the enjoyment scale – those that you loathe or perhaps like least.

So be honest, and don't worry if you end up with nothing with an H next to it. It may be time to rethink about your life's work or consider a career change. This has happened often when clients go through the exercise; usually, though, it serves as a reminder of why we do what we do, because all the stuff we love is ranked H is a disproportionately small proportion of all that we do. Most importantly, we can see that there is a spread, and where there is a spread there is the potential for delegation.

Between the first and second columns we now have paired rankings, the second for dependency and the third for enjoyment. Clearly, those tasks with an LL next to them are the ones to focus on first. These are the areas least enjoyed and with the least dependency are the easiest to delegate to start with.

Task List Profile with timings

The next stage is either to give thought to the length of time required to complete each task if it is repetitive or at least to estimate the amount of time a person (if not you) would need to attend to it. This is useful in a number of ways. First, when it is a task that is not one you particularly love, it actually takes you a greater length of time to achieve it than a task that you enjoy.

We all prevaricate when forced to do something that doesn't make us tick and I've documented that previously in this book, but the fact that you now have to consider how much time someone who is more suited to the task will need, puts into stark contrast how long you would take if you kept the task to yourself.

Second, when you look at it as a task for someone else, you inevitably start to think about by whom or how this could be done and, third, you start to realize just how much of your own time is going to be released once you have dispensed with this area of your working life.

In addition, there are other benefits; once you rid yourself of this shoulder-sinker, you are able to view it from a different angle and will probably be far more able to contribute to its development and play to your strengths than you might have been when down in the mire with it. Let me illustrate:

A case in point here are some items listed on my own Task Profile, that of the business's month end process and accounts Sage entry and credit control. The first took days to complete; the second was usually left until it bunched up, deadlines loomed and we paid more to the accountant to 'journal' errors and omissions. It also meant no time for electronic bank reconciliation, which would have saved significant money on having the statements manually double-checked. The third item on my Task List Profile – credit control – was, frankly, very badly done: through the financial crisis, clients had either struggled to pay, gone bust owing too much money to the business or taken advantage of our lax ways and delayed payment for as long as they could get away with. I don't regard myself as a useless or incapable businessperson. I simply had too much on my plate and, ironically, my over-capability (i.e. my ability to work my way around the Sage program and prepare accounts) had led to my not having to delegate the accounting to someone else who would have not been so lax. Most devastating was the point when cash ran so dry that in spite of a debtor book worth tens of thousands of pounds there were insufficient funds to cover the salary payments.

In addition, I had attempted to delegate these tasks before, and part of the problem was that in doing so I had not kept my eye on the ball and realized how bad things had become and how poorly the records now were. My own somewhat time-consumed and not amazing time at the helm of the accounts hadn't been as bad as it could get and now it was in an even worse position. When I assess the episode against the delegation process I champion in this book, I conclude that I hadn't really done anything too wrong: I was clear on the 'why' (free up my time), the 'what' (all documented and process clear), the 'who' and the 'how'. In retrospect, two things had been lacking: a way of measuring success and being realistic about what we could achieve, which pivoted on one thing: communication. I thought I had the right person who could realistically achieve the role requirements which had very clear measures. In the communication, I was being told what I wanted to hear, and that was all I was hearing. My checking and reporting wasn't as tight as it ought to have been.

However, for me to take it all back would only have solved the short-term problem and so I felt I had to hold my nerve and to learn from this, which enabled the subsequent delegation to be far more successful.

So successful in fact that within six months all records were entirely up to date and fully system reconciled (something that we had never managed before), accounts were ready to be submitted at the half-year point, the whole process taking less than 50% of one person's time and all clients (of which there were hundreds every month) paid up to date. In addition, the management information that resulted within the team enabled a far more simplified and profitable pricing model to emerge. My involvement in this whole process was now reduced to no more than a couple of hours a month, which was all pleasurable, forward-thinking stuff.

One of the most rewarding parts of this process is to prioritize what you are going to delegate and add up how much time you will be left with. Now return to your 'why' and indulge yourself a little. There is now a way you can get this time back and do what you first visualized in your 'why'.

Task List Profile with 'who' column

Once you have gone through your Task Profile List, you will be able to identify 'who'. Needless to say, names are not necessary at this point. It may be an entirely new recruit. But what starts to form is a job description for one or more people or companies. We look in more depth at the 'who' in the next chapter.

Yuletide delegation – a New Year's resolution?[1]

The ultimate in delegation is: To only do what only you can do.

In a team, if everybody did that the result could be pictorially resembled by a Christmas tree, where the branches are the people and the baubles are the tasks.

Picture this then, at the bottom of the tree, the branches are bigger, longer and fatter (i.e. there are more people at this level). The baubles are bigger (i.e. the tasks can be done by more people).

As you move up the tree, the branches and the baubles reduce in size. This is because there are fewer people who are capable of the tasks represented by the baubles, presumably because the tasks are more difficult, require more decision-making ability or more authority, skill or experience etc.

Then, when you get to the top of the tree, the branches are small and few and far between, the baubles tiny. Finding top people able to operate at the top level is harder. There are fewer of them. And your decoration at

---

[1] From my blog at http://thegailthomas.blogspot.co.uk/2013/12/yuletide-delegation-festive-thought-for.html, accessed 10th October 2014.

the top of the tree – be it an angel, fairy, Santa, mega bauble or whatever – represents the one person with whom the buck stops. They are the focal point. When they get changed, it's very noticeable.

I remember once an MD who went on to become CEO of a major international organization saying to me, when I joked about his fat cat bank balance, in a most serious tone, that he was paid to make decisions that no one else in the organization could or would make. I paraphrase his words – which will stay with me forever – 'I am paid to take two or three good decisions every week, that's it, no one else could do it at the moment, and that makes me worth every penny I'm paid, even if I do nothing else.'

I agree entirely.

10
STEP 3: WHO TO DELEGATE TO

D elegation broaches many areas of professional expertise, and now we step on the shoes of recruitment as we think about the importance of 'who' in our delegation process.

The 'who' sits in front of the 'how' in this book and also in the process I take clients through when it comes to delegation, because if the 'who' is wrong, then successful delegation is less likely to happen. Being human completely gets in the way of selecting the right person and, in my opinion, so it should. Let me explain...

Over the years, both as a corporate manager and executive, and as a direct employer through my own businesses, whenever I have compromised – for whatever reason – on the recruitment for any role, I have largely paid the price. Naturally, there are many hoops to jump through, mechanisms for the measurement of a prospective employee, psychometric profiles, GMAT and a plethora of creative questions and riddles used to sift the wheat from the chaff and all have their place and are credible in their own way. They are variously employed within my own businesses, but for me the alchemy in recruitment is in the ability to predict the extent or even existence of a positive psychological contract.

I've heard it said that we recruit 'people like us' and I go for that every time. I do not want to do down the art of recruitment and the professionals involved in it as well as the psychology, expertise and erudition involved in this area of business operation. I do not reduce it into my own layman's speak or somewhat on occasion apparently laissez-faire approach to hiring people. But when I can find people I connect with, relate to, *get*; even when they are of very different character and approach to me, I get on better with them, they understand me more deeply, I open up to them in many ways (not least in terms of vulnerability and humour) and vice versa and communicate better with them as a result. In my experience, when this happens, you have a far better chance of understanding the common goal, what you are both aiming for and what makes both sides tick.

To add more gravitas to my point, I defer to this excellent summation from CIPD.

The psychological contract on the other hand looks at the reality of the situation as perceived by the parties, and may be more influential than the formal contract in affecting how employees behave from day to day. It is the psychological contract that effectively tells employees what they are required to do in order to meet their side of the bargain and what they can expect from their job. It may not – indeed in general it will not – be strictly enforceable...

A positive psychological contract typically supports a high level of employee engagement. However the concept of engagement goes beyond employees' attitudes and underlines the need for managers to draw out employees' discretionary behaviour.

Two-way communication, formal and informal, is essential as a form of reality check and a basis for building mutual trust.

More of which can be found at http://www.cipd.co.uk/hr-resources/factsheets/psychological-contract.aspx

As an MBA student I appreciated the informality of the theory of the psychological contract, but it is only as a student of delegation that I come to love it and live it, but I believe when it truly exists to the benefit of the organization it is in a much deeper form than the CIPD defines it.

The promises the employer is expected to give the employee as their side of the contract largely comprise pay and benefits, job and personal security, training, interesting tasks, feedback, recognition and promotion prospects.

To this end, in the same way that being clear about the 'why' is vital to the delegator it is vital to the delegation recipient. Whatever motivates them is their own concern but if they're able to be honest and open about it with their employer or line manager and the employer is able to fulfil the employee's 'why' through the achievement of the tasks and as a reward for that then that hackneyed phrase 'win–win situation' comes to mind.

THE GIFT OF TIME

In essence, to me the psychological contract is about a multitude of hackneyed phrases: hearts and minds, being on the same page, singing from the same ... it means that you get each other. Once unified in this way and clear about each other's motivations and those of the business then, put simply, delegation just works.

For me the psychological contract is about chemistry – no romanticism intended here, like a love affair – born of a desire to make each other happy (a couple or manager/employee), while also achieving the aims of those within the remit of the nearer context (nuclear family or team) and promoting the well-being and happiness of the far context (extended family or department) to the benefit of the wider context (community or organization).

To get back to the 'who' in our delegation pathway, it is important – as the CIPD extract emphasizes – to communicate well. Throughout this book and its associated learnings, I stress the importance of great communication (for 'great', read honest, open and frequent).

Gems start-up case study: Part 2

As a manufacturing business, being started up by a partnership that knew nothing at all about manufacturing, this business was ripe for delegation every which way right from the start. Also by virtue of lack of expertise of the founding team, it enables perfect illustration of how tasks which appear enjoyable and highly dependent on a novice still have to be delegated in order to play to the strengths both of suppliers and of team members and to get the job done.

We've gone through the 'why' of this business and if I refer to the past chapter on delegation stakeholders and the discussion on business-types complexity, Gems Lingerie is one that sits in the simplest and most straight-forward category. It is a product, after all. Naturally, it is slightly more complicated because it involves manufac-turing and all the requisite sourcing, transport and qual-ity assurance requirements that a straightforward re-seller agreement would not involve, but still its place is at the bot-tom of the pile in terms of its overall complexity as a direct sale.

Gems start-up Task List Profile

Function and task	D	E	Suppliers (who)
Product			
Design	M	H	1, A and B
Fabrics sourcing	L	M	1 and 6
Fabrics suppliers	L	L	2, 3, 4, 5
Pattern	L	L	6
Prototypes	L	H	6 and 7
Model fit	H no L!	H	8, 9, 10, 11, 12 A and B
Grading	L	L	6
Labelling	H	L	13

(Continued)

133

Function and task	D	E	Suppliers (who)
Manufacture	L	L	7
Quality assurance	H	L	14, A and B
Packaging	H	M	15
Transport			
To and from	L	L	16
Marketing			
Logo design	H	H	17
Website design	M	M	18
Website build	L	L	18
Ecommerce	L	L	19
Social media	M	H	20, A and B
Advertising	M	H	21, 22
PR	M	H	23
Sales			
Telephone orders	L	M	24
Payment	L	L	25
Processing	L	L	26
Operations			
Labelling (outer)	H	L	27
Pick and pack	L	L	28 A and B
Packaging	L	L	29
Fulfilment	L	L	28
Returns	L	L	28 A and B
Systems			
Stock control	L	L	A and B
Audit	L	L	31
Accounts	L	L	30, 31

(Continued)

Function and task	D	E	Suppliers (who)
Finance			
Grant aid	M	L	32
Banking	L	L	33
Governance			
Company formation	L	L	34
VAT registration	L	L	35

The bulk of the time involved in getting this business started was in the research and development of the product. It was vital that the product was right and with no soulmate UK precedent (i.e. being the first of its kind) it was this that would take the majority of the time to market. In essence, with this time taken out, the equivalent collapsed timeline for launch would be no more than three months.

In spite of this, when it came to the Task List Profile, there were some 34 headline (i.e. not yet broken down) tasks involving or requiring delegation to 35 different suppliers plus the founding team (A and B). This was for one single initial product and did not include any strategic or product development. This was purely my own Task List Profile; it did not reflect anyone else's or my partner's opinion. I did it quickly and instinctively, which is how the Task List Profile in the first instance should be done: without too much preparation. Otherwise, it becomes over-thought, over-engineered or even a shoulder-sinker! Mine is included here more to illustrate the points that follow.

We've already said that – by virtue of small tasks looming large, shoulder-sinkers and the importance of playing to joy and strengths – anything which ranks low on both the dependency and enjoyment scale should be first up for outsourcing. Let's take that as a given and analyse anything that falls outside of it:

L/M or M/L

In the Task List, this meant fabric sourcing (L/M), telephone orders (L/M) and grant aid (M/L). The first two were not dependent on the founders' skill sets and were easily handed over, but the will to do so was limited a little by the fact that they were enjoyable tasks in their own right (in my case, it's fun to spend some time (but not hours) on the Internet looking for suppliers and requesting and then receiving samples), but someone either more skilled than me, or at least with the know-how of fabrics and knowledge of UK suppliers, would do it (and quicker to boot), or it could be delegated to someone with even less knowledge than me with a clear brief.

Grant aid is a different matter. It is harder to delegate the requirements specification because it is more complicated and in our heads, but the form filling associated with dealing with the government-appointed bodies ... enough said, it finds itself low on the enjoyment scale.

M/M

Just one thing here on my list and that was website design. I am not a website designer, hence the M ranking. I clearly needed someone else to do that for me but it depended on my/our brief or vision of how the website would look and operate for our customers, so the dependency was not high, because, as a fairly straightforward retail website, one could argue that a Web designer with previous experience could arguably do a reasonable job even without a brief and using his or her daily working knowledge.

In terms of enjoyment, there were elements that were a pleasure: seeing how it looked and felt and the visual bits to be proud of as a business creator, but less appealing to me was the thought of checking site maps and thinking through the process. All do-able and within my capability but would I rather be creating a new product? H all the way!

L/H or H/L

The low dependence and high enjoyment tasks for me in this business start-up phase were the creation of the prototypes. The dependence was low because all it really required was a seamstress (which I am not) and we were lucky to have an extremely skilled one. That said, I loved seeing the pre-products being made and turning up for us to touch, feel and try and to show our friends and research groups.

Nice for me but the classic downside of an L/H task is distraction. It takes me away from doing stuff I ought to be doing that is dependent on me but that I possibly enjoy a little less. The good news was, though, that if I really wanted to learn to sew and create my own prototypes, I needed to focus on delegating anything that sat in the L (none at the moment), M or H dependency column but ranked less than H in terms of my enjoyment. Doing this would free up my time to indulge myself in doing more of the things I loved to do (i.e. in case it needs reiteration – the benefits of delegation), hence my change in the Task List Profile from H to L in the case of dependency on model fit. I originally ranked this task H because I was a model on whom the product was fitted (naturally, I want the product for myself as a customer) but I was not integral to getting the fit right – anyone can put on a pair of knickers! And so this task becomes low on its dependence, certainly on me and in all truth my business partner also.

H dependence and L enjoyment tasks are the hardest to delegate and I had a few in this category: inner-garment labelling (wash care instructions etc.), quality assurance (checking stitching, stretch and so on) and outer labelling (bar code) is just not my thing, but unless it's right it seriously affects the integrity of the product. If I/we was/were to delegate these things, these would have been the ones that took our time to think through, to recruit and select the right people to be involved in the process, the right measures for checking all was well – our reputation as a brand depended on it.

M/H and H/M

For me, much of the design and marketing sat in medium (M) dependence and high enjoyment (at least in the start-up phase). I could have input into the creative side but I was not an expert in spite of the fact that I loved this part, hence the M dependence.

With a clear strategy and plan (which again would involve us a lot – time – but enabled us to outsource the implementation once the business was launched by finding the right company or employee – time – who would get this done. This area, however, sat in the more strategic relationship that the founders had with their potential future exit, and hence the value of the business. For the time being, there were few reasons to delegate M/H tasks but they would become the priority if or when we started to consider selling the business or our exit from the day-to-day running of it.

H/M tasks such as product (not postage) packaging had a high dependence on the founders because they formed an integral part of the brand as a product extension (i.e. this was an add-on product sold separately). For me it was not a total downer, nor was it a total boat-floater to bring it to market. This was the hardest category to delegate after H/L in terms of practicality (versus emotion, see H/H to follow) because the dependence was so high and because it was not so bad to do (medium enjoyment). It is easier to take back into one's own inbox if things don't go smoothly in the delegation process.

H/H

This is 'the zone', or where one finds oneself operating in one's 'flame'. There are many positive adjectives to describe this feeling, when you are doing what you love and your business, job, family or whoever needs you to be doing this because it's what you do best. Joy cubed. However, as we have touched upon, when it comes to reluctant retirement or, more likely, a healthy exit, these are the parts that become the most essential to delegate well, as the likelihood is, in the case of a business exit, they will be what gives the business its vital point of difference. In the case of a career change or move, this area of your role becomes your legacy and it may be tempting to leave the firm or team in the lurch without your valuable expertise and abilities (a stroke of the ego on the back of those 'It's not the same without . . . ' laments), but to delegate this successfully means you can also take pride in leaving the place in great shape to continue what you did and how you did it but also in a position to improve upon it, which is a much better legacy all round.

Delegation and the team

While many of the principles of delegation apply on a one-to-one basis as well as to the team as a whole, it applies slightly less clearly when delegating to a new team whose members have not worked with you or each other before.

This is different from the notion of being a new leader. This is the opposite. It is about being part of and leading an entirely new team put together for the specific role of taking on your delegated work or aims. It therefore feels relevant here for me to include the thoughts of my colleague and team expert Tamsen Garrie. My reasoning here is that in the context of successful or unsuccessful delegation there are team dynamics at play. Sometimes even when all parts of the delegation process have been executed well and with all due consideration to all that this book holds dear (including team members playing to their apparent strengths), a new set of people required to work together, even with the most pristine of procedural instruction and accompanying training, can present as a gaggle of warring politicians when they're new. A team that doesn't work is simply a bunch of people and they can feel as related as the members of a bus queue until they start to *get* each other and find their place and feel their space.

There are recognized theories on team dynamics and I am fond of one put forward by Tuckman.[1] I've seen his theory in action as a team player and as a manager and entrepreneur. Tamsen, in her extensive work with clients from a diverse range of companies, establishments and industries, adapts Tuckman and applies its learnings to help teams perform better, sooner. Her observations are fascinating and she shares a snapshot of her expertise here.

Building an aligned team

Effective delegation in the context of the team relies heavily on the extent to which the team is aligned – both with the

---

[1] http://www.businessballs.com/tuckmanformingstormingnormingperforming. htm, accessed 10th October 2010.

vision, culture and goals of the team and with each other in terms of attitude and attributes, skills and strengths, and roles and responsibilities.

The word 'team' is often used to describe a group of people who work together. However, there is a big difference between a work group and a team.

Whereas a work group is a collection of individuals who *coordinate their individual efforts*, a team is a group of people who work together *collectively* towards a *shared vision*.

This distinction between a work group and a team is important because while a team will always achieve more consistent, more significant and more long-term results than a work group it is much more difficult to build.

Building a team requires the commitment and the capacity on the part of the leader to facilitate a natural four-stage process of team development and, owing to the nature of their role within that process, to also develop themselves as a leader throughout the various stages.

A work group has an individual and *independent* focus. The emphasis is on the individuals within the group rather than the group as a whole. An individual who works as part of a work group may have goals, clarity of tasks and responsibilities, and accountability for outcomes, but while they may come together with the rest of the group, it is usually with the sole purpose of sharing information as it is their leader/manager that they ultimately look to for direction and guidance.

A team, on the other hand, has a collective and *interdependent* focus. While the individuals in the team are highly valued, the emphasis is on the group as a whole. Personal agendas are also team agendas and collective success takes priority over individual success. People who work as part of a team have a strong sense of shared purpose because their roles and responsibilities are defined by the team's vision and goals and while they each have their own roles, they have *shared* responsibility for outcomes, which means that they depend heavily on each other to perform their respective roles well. Members of a team come together frequently and with far greater purpose than simply to communicate: they discuss challenges and problems, brainstorm solutions, share ideas, plan work and make joint decisions. People in a team do not look solely to the leader/manager for direction or for guidance; they look to each other and so their accountability for outcomes is provided by the team as a whole.

When you successfully leverage *interdependence* in a group, you have a team and when you have a team, the overall achievement is far greater than the sum of the individuals within it.

Together > Everyone > Achieves > More

So how do you build a team?

There's an approach that I have developed called the Team Alignment Method™ which I use with my clients

THE GIFT OF TIME

to build an aligned team. However, before I share that, it is important first to understand the natural four-stage process that a group always goes through en route to becoming a team.

Gail mentioned the Team Development Model developed by Bruce Tuckman in 1965, which details the four stages that all teams go through.

He calls it: Forming > Storming > Norming > Performing.

While this model has been around for many years and has been proven to be effective in its application, I have adapted it to suit the modern business world and my preferred emphasis on interdependence. However, while my labelling and explanation of the stages is slightly different from Tuckman's, the essence remains very true to his original work.

The Team Development Model

Stage 1 – Starting

In this stage, the *starting* of the team takes place and the individual's behaviour is driven by the simple desire to be accepted. There is a lack of understanding of the team's vision or purpose and there is high dependence on the leader/manager for direction and guidance.

This stage tends to be comfortable for the individuals as they behave and work relatively independently. The focus tends to be on goals and tasks and on who does what and when, in addition to gathering information about and forming impressions of each other.

To the leader/manager, the team may appear to be working well as delegated tasks are completed. However, the reality is that often they are not completed as effectively or as efficiently as they could be and the avoidance of any conflict means that issues and feelings are not addressed. As a result mutual respect and trust are not established and so success it limited.

The starting stage is an important stage as it allows the members of the team to get to know one another, both on a personal level and in terms of their preferences and how they respond under pressure. Relationships begin to form in this stage.

Stage 2 – Kicking

In this stage, the *kicking* of the team occurs as, while the vision and the purpose of the team becomes clearer, uncertainty about where the individuals fit into that builds. They begin to vie for position, to assert their preferences and to impose their ideas, and as differences are emphasized, tension arises and conflict and arguments can occur.

This stage is not avoidable. All teams go through this stage and, for a team that has never worked together before, it is especially significant. Owing to the often contentious nature of this stage, it can feel uncomfortable, especially for those who are particularly averse to conflict, as individuals air and explore their differences.

For the leader/manager, delegation at this stage is a challenge as the individuals shift responsibility for tasks and outcomes and apportion blame for failings.

The kicking stage is an essential stage as it creates the conditions to enable the individuals to push through their differences by both recognizing and accepting them. It enables them to identify where they and each other member brings value to the team and to begin to establish mutual understanding and respect. It does, however, have the potential to be a destructive stage if there is a lack of tolerance and patience. Cliques may form at this stage and power struggles may occur. However, with the freedom to share opinions and feelings openly and without judgement, the team are able to work together more comfortably. Some teams unfortunately never develop past this stage.

Stage 3 – Working

In this stage, the *working* of the team begins as agreement replaces resistance and the individuals find commonality and ways in which they complement each other. They begin to compromise their own agendas for the benefit of the team as a collective. Their desire for and their commitment to the team's success is strong and they begin to depend more on each other than on the manager and to work together, playing to their strengths and pulling on the strengths of their teammates.

This stage is a welcome stage for everyone after they've been in *kicking* and it is highly noticeable as tension and conflict are replaced by mutual appreciation and respect, and trust builds.

For the leader/manager, a deeper level of delegation is possible as the team appear to get what they are about and are both willing and able to take on more responsibility.

The working stage is significant as everyone becomes clear not just on the role they play and the value they bring but also on the value brought by every individual in the team. Everyone begins to feel appreciated and supported and this is reflected in the outcomes they achieve. Some individuals may continue to operate independently on occasion, and ideas, opinions and feelings may not be shared openly in this stage for fear of recreating conflict.

Stage 4 – Rocking

In this stage, the *rocking* of the team emerges as the individuals cease to operate independently and instead operate interdependently, depending on each other to perform their respective roles well. There is complete openness, high empathy, mutual respect and trust, and as a result the team proactively and collectively seek ways of getting the work done efficiently and effectively without the need for external leadership or management.

The individuals are knowledgeable and competent, highly motivated and dependent on each other, which makes collective problem solving and decision making easy. What is most evident in this stage is that differing ideas, opinions and feelings are both encouraged and welcomed with the intention of challenging the norm and continually finding new solutions and ways forward.

For the leader/manager, delegating to this team is not only easier but also a joy! The individuals are clear about where they are heading, they understand the role they play in the bigger picture and they are confident in playing to their strengths to perform that role well. Equally, their skills and strengths, roles and responsibilities and their attitude and attributes complement and support both each other and the team's vision, culture and goals. They fully appreciate the importance of being delegated to in the context of the vision and they thrive as a result of the increase in expectation and responsibility.

The rocking stage is the stage to aspire to because this is stage when the team dynamics become highly functional, the individuals within the team thoroughly enjoy the experience of working together and they really power forward with what feels like ease. Momentum builds and achieving the team's vision becomes inevitable.

Relapsing

Team development is not a linear process. Even the most rocking teams will experience challenges and may revert to earlier stages in the cycle when changes occur.

The loss of a valued member, the addition of someone new, a change in leadership or direction and focus or even the achievement of a significant goal can result in a relapse. Most typically, the team will revert to *kicking* as new agendas, ideas, perspectives and opinions challenge the existing dynamics of the team.

For the leader/manager, delegation can suffer in the face of a relapse as the impact on communication results in mistakes or missed deadlines.

However, a previously rocking team that has fully experienced what it is to work interdependently, already possesses the characteristics required to adapt to the changes, address the challenges and to progress through the process quickly and with relative ease. A team in the working stage may struggle with this and a kicking team may never recover, which is why aspiring to create a rocking team is so important.

The role of the leader

I talked at the beginning about the importance of team alignment in the context of effective delegation. An aligned team is simply a team that has progressed successfully through the team development process and that possesses all of the qualities detailed in the rocking stage. In summary, they know where they are going (the vision), how they behave (the culture), what they are aiming for (the goals) and how they fit in (the roles).

While I have referred to the team development process as a natural one, the transition from starting to kicking to working to rocking does not occur by accident and, as I also said earlier, requires the commitment and the capacity on the part of the leader to both facilitate the process and to develop themselves as a leader throughout the stages.

It is the leader's role to facilitate the team development process and to create and nurture the conditions to enable the individuals within the team to move through the stages incrementally and without perceived threat to themselves personally.

I call this 'Hot Frogging' and I recommend all team leaders that I work with adopt the approach of Hot Frogging when facilitating and managing any kind of change.

The term originates from the following well-known anecdote that describes the inability of people to react to significant changes when they occur *gradually*.

If a frog is placed directly into boiling water, it perceives a threat immediately and will jump right out. However, if a frog is placed in cold water that is then gradually heated, it becomes accustomed to the heat over time, adapts to the new conditions and will remain in the pot willingly.

Now, it's not a particularly kind analogy and I prefer to think that the frog is eventually removed from the pot before it boils to death(!), but it does, I hope, underline the point I'm making.

If a leader attempted to impose their desire for the team to work interdependently too quickly, the individuals in the team (the frogs!) would be likely to jump. It is human nature – we do not like change and we are often threatened by the unknown. However, if a leader accepts that the journey to their desired destination is a process and that their role as leader is to guide and support the team through that process, they are far more likely to reach their desired destination.

To facilitate this journey, there is a method that I developed a number of years ago to take leaders and their teams from 'starting' to 'kicking' to 'working' to 'rocking'. I find that by approaching team alignment in this way the transition occurs organically.

It really is a joy to witness!

The Team Alignment Method™

Step 1: Create the vision (where we are going)

As you know, one of the key characteristics of a rocking team is that they work interdependently towards a shared vision.

A vision is simply a picture created in the imagination and in this context it is a picture of how the team want things to be in the future. It provides a destination to which the team can move towards together. Without a shared vision, creating a rocking team is simply not possible, because shared vision is the glue that binds the individuals in the team together.

So, creating the team's vision is essential but what is equally important is involving the team in the creation of it. This is because when the individuals in the team are involved in deciding on the direction they are going and, importantly, defining 'why', they *choose* to be committed and motivated and when they are committed and motivated through *choice*, a fully engaged team emerges, complete with a strong sense of camaraderie, mutual obligation and peer-to-peer pressure which establishes accountability of the self-policing kind.

As a result, the leader goes from managing the individuals in the team to managing the team as a collective, which in turn then manages the individuals within it. In effect, the leader delegates the day-to-day management of the team to the team itself.

Step 2: Decide on the culture (how we behave)

While the vision provides the direction, it is the team culture that provides the conditions to enable the team to achieve it.

Culture is often difficult to define because it is not tangible. However, culture is entirely visible through its manifestation in the work environment: in the behaviour of the people in the team.

I describe culture as a personality. In a person, personality is a construct of their mindset (beliefs, values and attitude) and their behaviour. Equally, a team's culture is a construct of their collective mindset and the behaviour which results when the team agree to and comply with a set of guidelines for working together.

Culture literally translates to 'How we behave around here', and the more explicit the team is about the culture that best supports the vision the more likely they are to adopt consistent behaviour that also supports it. Naturally, the more involved the team are in deciding the culture, the more they own it and the more they then 'live' it.

Step 3: Establish the goals (what we are aiming for)

While the vision provides direction and the culture provides the conditions to enable the team to achieve it, it is the team's goals that drive their daily, weekly and monthly activities to ensure that they move incrementally and consistently towards it.

The vision is the destination. However, often by the nature of a vision, the destination is a long way in the future. Therefore aiming for the destination on a daily, weekly or monthly basis can be overwhelming. The goals bring the vision closer to the current reality, providing achievable milestones to aspire to and reach along the way.

Again, the more involved the team are in establishing the goals, the more committed they are to doing whatever it takes to achieve them.

Step 4: Define the roles (how we fit in)

One of the most important characteristics of a rocking team is that each individual within it is completely clear

THE GIFT OF TIME

about the role they play in achieving their common goals and reaching their shared vision. As a result, they have a high level of accountability.

'Accountability' is often described as being responsible for something when, actually, that is what 'responsibility' means. Accountability is not just about being responsible for something: it's about being answerable for it, too, and the distinction between the two things is an important one.

Answerability is incredibly powerful, because when someone else's interest in an individual achieving or completing something, be it a task or a goal, translates to their actively ensuring that they do, the individual achieves much more and faster.

However, accountability only works when there is complete clarity of responsibility and expectations and this is why defining the individual roles within the team, complete with where responsibility lies for specific tasks and who is accountable for certain outcomes, is absolutely essential.

In doing this, the leader works with the team to allocate responsibility for tasks and outcomes to individuals within the team based on their strengths. Now this is where many leaders and managers get it wrong. We have come to believe that our strengths are the things we can do well, which is why so many of us find ourselves on a career path that we later come to dislike. The thing is your strength is *not* the thing you do can do well. Your strength is not the thing you're good at. That is your *skill*. Your strength is the thing you are good at *and* you enjoy doing. It's the thing you are good at *and* energized by. It's the thing that makes you feel *strong*. That is your *real* strength

When the individuals within the team are allocated tasks and responsibilities based on their *real* strengths, that's when things start to get interesting.

Building the team

By leading the team through the Team Alignment Method step by step, even the most inexperienced team leader can move their team from starting to rocking. What is more important than experience is strong facilitation skills and belief in the process.

By starting with step one: the vision, followed by step two: the culture, most groups will transition from starting into kicking relatively quickly as deciding where they are heading and defining their collective values throws up all sorts of issues.

Successfully leading the group through step two and into step three is the key to getting them out of kicking and into working, as a kicking team will struggle to establish common goals.

The rocking stage emerges only when the team have successfully worked through both step three and step four and this can take some time. In fact, many teams remain in working and the impact on effective delegation is that the

THE GIFT OF TIME

leader is still required to direct and manage the individuals in the team.

Only when the leader and the team commit entirely to the Team Alignment Method can the impact of effective delegation be fully realized in a team that is self-managed.

The impact of this was demonstrated in the results of a team I worked with recently in the creative sector. The leader engaged me to support him in creating a new team for the specific purpose of developing and marketing a new product. Some of the individuals within the new team knew of some of the other members, but only two had actually worked together before so we really were starting at *starting.*

Over three weeks, I worked with the leader and his team using the Team Alignment Method. The client was a strong leader who instilled confidence naturally, and he had selected these people himself, so naturally they, for the most part, shared some common values and aspirations. Therefore, aside from a couple of contentions, step one and step two were pretty painless.

However, as we got into step three: the goals, the kicking stage occurred as half the group preferred to approach the project in one way and half the group in the opposite way. The leader could see the value in both approaches and so our job was to create the conditions to enable the group to discuss the two options openly and without judgement and to agree a mutual way forward. This involved a number of further communications, both in person and via email, and from the contention, a third, more preferable approach emerged. What was interesting was that the opposing sides both recognized they would have been unlikely to have seen the third option had they not experienced the initial conflict. It was as a result of the conflicting ideas and opinions that many of the individuals' strengths became apparent which made step four: the roles a relatively simple step in comparison and that rocking team went on to create one of the most successfully marketed products, with the highest profits that the company had ever seen.

Teams are a complicated thing; simply managing a group of humans to perform decently together is tremendously tricky, even for the most experienced of leaders, let alone motivating them to *rock* in an independent way.

Tamsen's methods are pragmatic and, I find, calming and reassuring, because there is a precedent a leader can look to and take confidence from. Delegation requires huge trust, especially when one's own performance or, arguably more risky, one's own business' performance (not to mention brand and reputation) is on the line. So when things appear to be going wrong, it is a natural response to panic and start to take work back, to not trust things will get done or believing mistakes will be made. It is important at this stage for a leader to think and retain a delegation mindset, to hold their nerve to manage the energy, focus and direction of the team through its agreed culture, goals and

THE GIFT OF TIME

aims as well as to manage their own energy and emotion and avoid being dragged down into the realms of lost confidence and short-term thinking.

This takes courage and faith. It is a big reason why I was motivated to write this book. One can easily fall out with delegation because of other factors and barriers, many of which have been mentioned already in this book, but when it comes to team dynamics, it is easy to muddy the waters and assume that somehow it is the leader who has delegated or managed badly, when in fact, as Tamsen points out and rightly concludes, such discord amongst within team is simply part of the process.

Tamsen's focus is on the team dynamic here. She makes it clear that the leader has clear requirements of him or her through the stages of team development. Should you choose to further your knowledge of her work, she also delves into the symptoms and remedies of each team stage. My fascination lies in this area. It is so very practical and so very reassuring from a confidence per- spective that, as a delegator, it isn't necessarily your delegation that will cause this angst, you haven't made a sure-fire mistake, but you nonetheless have to be well equipped and emotionally strong to deal with it and pull the team through.

When I align my own theory and experience with Tamsen's over-view and overlay the delegation Venn diagram (Figure 12.1) on, in particular, the *kicking* phase of team development, I see huge synergy in our thinking. When cliques and strong opinions form in the first instance, it is distressing for the leader. They know what they are meant to do but if this is expected it can throw the leadership dynamic as much as the team one. It can result in a different response from the leader too, depending on their instinct, emotion and/or delegation type indicator profile. Mostly the team is at risk of the *delegation* and responsibility being taken away from them: their behaviour suggests they might not be trustworthy. If the leader loses their confidence, or feels ineffective in their attempts to unite the team, quality and frequency of *communication* can be affected. Where the manager begins to abdicate or at least avoid the conflict, the feedback loop becomes lost, and a move away from agreed protocol and standards of operation (*process*) results as the manager stops managing and the team's divisive situation influences their approach to their work.

Much of the latter is mitigated if the team play to their strengths, which Tamsen rightly defines as something which combines both enjoyment and skill. I agree wholeheartedly and firmly believe that when the team is genuinely recruited to this prerogative, and the manager has delegated properly according to a Task List Profile (as opposed to a linear job description), to pick up on Tamsen's somewhat unpalatable analogy, it is amazing actually how fast you can boil a proverbial frog. Things are more liable to pull together and rock if no one involved (including the leader) can disagree with the fact that they love what they have been asked to do.

11
STEP 4: GETTING FROM 'I DO' TO 'YOU DO'

In its most basic form, delegation is the process from getting from 'I do' to 'You do' and is a movement away from *doing the work* to *ensuring that the work gets done*. There are three stages between the two which are iterative and may need to be revisited from time to time as a refresher, and they are:

I DO → I DO, YOU WATCH[1] → WE DO[2] → YOU DO, I WATCH[3] → YOU DO

   1   2   3   4   5

Naturally, this is simplified to prove a point, but the process holds whether it reflects the transition of one task or many and it always takes *time*.

Skipping from stage 1 to stage 5 without much in between reflects abdication, or 'dumping', rather than delegating, either

---

[1] Repeat as necessary.
[2] Loop back to previous step if need be.
[3] Go back to the first step if necessary.

through laziness, lack of time or lack of knowing how to delegate to best effect.

Stopping at stage 4 results in micro-managing, which is typical where a lack of trust or a need for control is a barrier. This is naturally demotivating to staff and fails to allow them to take responsibility for their own actions, learn how to do things for themselves, and means that organizations miss out on the improvement the (especially but not exclusively) fresh team members can contribute to an operational process or way of doing things.

Failing to move past stage 3 is clearly a duplication of effort, which affects the costs involved in the business through increased resources. This may happen as a result of guilt (manager does not feel the employee will enjoy the work), trust or control (just can't let go) or a lack of confidence in their own ability to hand over (know-how) or even to do the job itself. Ironically, both parties may actually enjoy such a joint effort, but in truth delegation isn't happening and the notion of it is extremely devalued.

It follows then at times that everything comes to a halt at stage 2 and an un-empowered, un-enthused employee is forced to become a bystander. Perhaps some can cope with this but the majority get bored and find something else to do or leave.

I certainly in my career as an employee, manager, businessperson and employer have seen all of these stages manifest, at every level in an organization. So while the basic premise of getting from 'I do' to 'You do' may seem incredibly simple, it is deceptively difficult to achieve and represents a classic case of the seemingly easiest things tripping up the most promising leaders and businesses.

Those that achieve it, though, especially if and when they support it with a 'to only do what only I can do' goal, know that it is entirely iterative and a constant habit or process that must be regularly revisited in a programme of checks and feedback mechanism (see Chapter 13). They have in addition been through a significant period of 'how' in terms of thinking through how best to achieve stage 5, which we tackle next.

12
STEP 5: HOW TO DELEGATE

So you're clear on 'why', have decided on 'what' and recruited the right 'who'. The process on moving from 'I do' to 'You do' is clear and 'how' comes next. It is process led, time consuming but vitally important. Its importance is such that it explains why there is so much documentation out there on 'how' to delegate. My belief is that delegation is broader than that and advice which dives straight into how is missing out on the vital pre-process which starts with clarity on 'why', 'what' and 'who' but most importantly the 'why', which is usually centred around value and benefits which in turn are broken down into value and benefits to the individual, to the team, to the business/organization/family. A firm understanding of why delegation would be good leads to having a far better chance of going well and achieving its aims.

So, down to the 'how', which very deliberately sits towards the back of this book. If a manager or business owner also understands what their barriers are or may be to delegation and how that sits within their management personality, they can ensure that the 'how' part accommodates those concerns or areas of weakness experienced during past delegation or, indeed, when they have been delegated to themselves. In my approach, I assume that in starting with 'why', deciding 'what' and selecting or finding 'who', the delegator has driven the process rather than reacted to a current level of workload. I assume that the motivation to delegate is a longer-term gain. I do so because successful delegation takes time, planning and thought and if it is an urgent requirement for help, though the same principles of course apply, the motivation may come from a different point in the process.

Delegate with confidence and get guilt out of the way

At this point, therefore, it is important for me to reiterate a need for confident delegation: you have every right to delegate because you and the recipient are clear 'why' it is important, you are clear on 'what' needs to be delegated and therefore the 'who' sitting in front of you has been chosen for their skills and strengths. This, therefore, negates the need for any guilt in handing over work. You are not begging a favour here: you are paying an appropriate person a fair fee for work they are capable of doing. If you're handing over work by way of an apology, you are devaluing their work before they've even begun. 'I'm sorry to do this to you' says that they are the wrong person, they're not going to love it or you're not otherwise playing to their strengths or rightful position in the organization. Naturally, there are times when the delegation may be unexpected or something new to them, but again if they are right, and given all they need to do the best job, as detailed in this chapter, there should be nothing to worry about.

Tools required for effective delegation

Google 'delegation' and you're bound to come up with the SMART acronym somewhere along the line. It's not a bad way to go but to me it feels a bit forced, as if the word comes first and the content later, but the principles do hold so if it's easier to remember it as Specific, Measurable, Achievable (or Agreed), Realistic (or Reported/Recorded) and Time-bound, then go for your life.

'How to delegate' is the bit that takes the most time, though it still incorporates much of the work that has been done prior to arrival at this point. It means thinking through and documenting the requirements and processes, systems and instructions, expectations and standards needed to do the job or task well. Team members or others willing to help need to be clear on what they are required to do. It's as simple as that. Table 12.1 has a breakdown.

It's been said and reiterated that time is the biggest barrier to delegation and the 'how' is one of the reasons why, especially if much of the 'how' is carried around in heads rather than down on paper or documented somehow or is otherwise easily transferrable. It takes effort to devise appropriate training, instruction or briefing and even more time to support that with appropriate, accurate and comprehensive documentation or procedures. It ends up being 'easier' or 'quicker' to do it oneself.

Table 12.1   Breaking down delegation.

What the delegator and delegated need to understand before starting	How this is made clear[1]
Why does this need to be delegated?	Business strategy or vision document/ business plan/job descriptions[2]/ communication on rewards for achievement and individual development aims
What is it that needs to be delegated?	Job description, role specification, team goals
Who is the person who will be doing the work?	People and job specification, recruitment methods and strategy, retention plans
How does the job get done?	Training/operations manuals, standard operating procedures (SOPs), performance management and measurements
What are the standards that are expected to be achieved?	As above with specifics on service levels and consequences of not achieving them as well as feedback channels if extra support is required
When is the work required by/what are the timescales involved?	Job description, role specification, team goals, SOPs, manuals, management and other reports
How much authority, responsibility and accountability do they have?	People and person specification, structure chart, job description, manuals and SOPs and the psychological contract

(Continued)

What the delegator and delegated need to understand before starting	How this is made clear[1]
What feedback mechanisms are in place to support the achievement *for both parties*?	One-to-one meetings, team meetings, performance management and reviews[3]

1. Each of these items is rarely relied upon in isolation and usually forms part of the overall continued communication.
2. Job description plural because, unless you're at risk of divulging state secrets, the more job descriptions the team can see, including those of their superiors, the better.
3. Feedback and management of delegation is so important that I devote a whole chapter to it separately from the topic of how to delegate to emphasize its critical nature and the importance of getting it right.

Be prepared for cock-ups

And by that I mean think through the worst-case scenarios as much as, and as soon as, possible, and plan accordingly. This is where past mistakes and poor experiences with regard to delegation suddenly become your friends as they help you to plan for the future with the benefit of hindsight.

Preparing in this way is not just good for business; it is also good for the delegation process. Almost the worst thing that can happen is that the work is taken back by the manager, who adds it back into their own workload and pulls the equivalent of an all-nighter to get the job done. Yes, the job is done, but where does that leave the stakeholders involved? The employee could be left feeling like a failure, the manager certainly tired, probably stressed and possibly reluctant to delegate again.

If the errors, mishaps or even disasters are thought about in advance (more time, I know) and a plan of action already documented and made clear, it has multiple benefits. First and vitally for the business, there is a clear way to remedy this situation and get back on track. Second, there is a way that the employee can understand the ramifications of what went wrong, why it went wrong and how to avoid this in the future. They also know what to do potentially or at least in part if the same thing happens again, either to them or when they delegate in the future. And finally, which is always a bonus, they may think of a way to improve the process as a whole or avoid the error going forward.

The Figure 12.1 shows that more or less all delegation issues are resolved through communication (of why, what, who, when, how) and/or process (how).

The delegation Venn diagram

This is a useful summary of delegation and all that is encompassed in how to do it well, how to troubleshoot if things are not going so well and how to overcome any barriers which prevent delegation perpetuating successfully.

Even if you don't read this book cover to cover, I suggest you look carefully at this model. You will gain a great deal of information about the art of delegation from it.

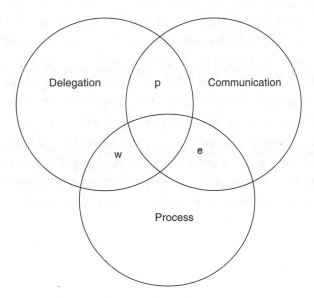

Figure 12.1   Delegation Venn diagram

Here's the top line Venn of delegation:

Successful delegation essentially has three parts:

- the **Delegation** itself, that is the act of actually handing things over to someone else to look after (effectively to use the terminology we're already familiar with in this book – the 'what' and the 'who';

- the **Communication** that underpins the need for delegation to happen – or the 'why';

- the **Process** that is required to ensure the work is done well and the feedback mechanisms are in place to keep it all on track.

Combine these three and there's a good chance all is going well, if not exceedingly well. This is represented by the centre part of the diagram, where the balance of all three elements is right. Where this balance is achieved, the manager is free to focus on using their own strengths and the team is operating at comfortable stretch with clear strategy, process and communication. The team are clear on what is required of them and why it will help the business, feel supported, well equipped and adequately trained to achieve to at least the required standard.

The Venn diagram also serves as an illustrative troubleshooter of what may be lacking if things don't feel right.

The area marked 'e' is where many may start when they pick up this book. Procedures and processes are likely to be established, though possibly not written down or documented in any way – in the case of a business owner, such details may still reside inside heads only, in a large business, team operations may be clear and available but not necessarily authorized as part of less senior roles. The need for delegation may be clear – certainly, the case for it will be apparent. Change is clearly required. The need for greater team support, managers or leaders to lead more convincingly or to greater ends is clear and pretty much understood. The manager or owner needs to let go, allow the handover to happen, and give permission for the team/support to take over and physically be responsible. This could be a result of ignorance (know-how), a lack of available resources (money) or a lack of certainty around what could result (trust/control) or a lack of time. Symptoms may include boredom, clock-watching and maybe a turnover of promising staff and a surprisingly high retention rate of the poorer performers.

Area 'w' sees a classic situation where delegation happens, processes are clear but there is a significantly sizeable information gap to cause a problem. Processes are disregarded, standards may not be met and morale may be low as work is perceived as drudging or undervalued. This is textbook 'corporate' territory, day-to-day seasonal and somewhat repetitive stuff, with no real change or understanding of the impact that their work truly has on the organization. It's tricky to manage, as any internal communications expert will attest, the need for honest communication, true company motives and plans become essential to colour in the monotone outline of what a business may stand for and what it truly needs to unite its workforce into empowered productivity with clear aims (and rewards) for initiative, development and progress in a mutually beneficial direction.

Area 'p' is close to my heart because I have seen this so many times in many of the thousands of clients that have come, gone, and stayed over the years. Here are those that understand the need to delegate: they want it, they need it and they are great at communicating how they need it fast because of what it will mean to them and their business. I understand these people and businesses most because I suspect I am just like them at heart if not – I hope – in practice. What is lacking here is process, training and support – the skill and tools needed to complete the 'how' to hand over workload from one to another. Time is of the essence here. There is no escaping the need to sit down and document the operational processes, ensure the systems are resilient and devise or buy the required training for the team or outsourced supplier/account manager or new recruit to understand thoroughly what they are required to do and how they get it done. This is time-taking, grind-through work which demands attention to detail, patience and testing. Even then, it is so open to interpretation that things inevitably go wrong from time to time, coupled with the fact that the unexpected happens (after all we're talking systems, manuals and people here; it could only be more fraught if it included animals and children!).

It's a useful exercise to plot one's personal and business position within the three parameters to understand the factors affecting successful delegation and bridge the gap accordingly. As a result, one can be 'high p' or 'w/p', 'low e' etc.

Without labouring the point, however, it is useful to note that wherever you sit or your business sits on the 'pew' (Process/Empower/Why) scale, time will be a major factor in your course correction. If the use of successful delegation can be analogized to being akin to a muscle, you have to exercise it evenly in a number of directions to achieve optimum use.

In conclusion, I would like to touch again on the psychological contract because it reflects the touchy-feely difference between the de rigueur terminologies that are 'responsibility' and 'accountability'. In Oxford dictionary terms, I can find no discernible difference between the two definitions, unless there is something there too subtle for my brash interpretation. In business terms, however, if you google it you'll no doubt find the same articles and references as I did. I think one is meant to assume that to be accountable is to somehow be more responsible for something that happens. That is to suggest that if the person responsible for the task or job messes it up, there is a person 'above' or 'behind' them who is therefore accountable, and in some cases of public office required to lose their job as a result. It would appear safe to assume, then, that the person accountable is the person with whom the buck stops. If that's right, I've no problem with it as an interpretation of the definition as it helps to illustrate the relative strength of the psychological contract.

Where communication and mutual understanding, aims, goals and values are clear and universally shared within the team (i.e. everyone is of the same mind), the psychological contract is naturally strong and every team member feels supported and equally responsible for the output of the group. This is especially the case for the leader of the team, who does (or very much should) accept and understand whose head is ultimately on the block, but who feels the huge support of a team, single supplier or employee when a strong psychological contract exists. Moving forward in this scenario is easy and smooth. In simple terms, someone has your back – and that's always a nice feeling.

The mirror of this, which we'll address more deeply in the next chapter but is important to touch on here, is the issue of giving credit where credit is due. Delegation truly backfires when the manager takes all the credit. While it may suggest that true accountability entitles a manager to do this, the smartest managers know that they look so much like a great leader when they're big enough to stand aside and let those they managed, developed and trusted to be delegated to do a great job for them.

Check, check, report

Delegation is a management tool or skill. In my opinion, it is an essential one. The keyword in the first sentence is 'management'. In order to achieve successful delegation, one has to manage it. That isn't to say one has to micro-manage it. Indeed, as I've said before, we all recognize that making mistakes is a great way to learn and delegation means allowing, in certain cases, that to happen in order to reinforce the message, but it all, nonetheless, has to be managed. To do anything less is to abdicate responsibility, and that is rarely a good context in which to operate.

The key is to plan, which, as I keep saying, takes time. Plan for the worst to happen and plan how to mitigate it if it does. Check, check, report is a highly summarized version of the 'situation confirmation' process (Figure 12.2).

The first 'check' in this process is the one that the delegator controls and ensures takes place. This may be deliberately liberal (allow a freer rein) or conservative (wary of errors or problems), that is to say, a more relaxed and casual update versus a more defined or detailed report or meeting feedback.

Regardless, what is essential here is some form of anticipation or 'what if' scenario (and probably more than one scenario will

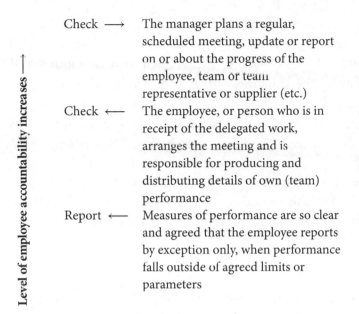

Level of employee accountability increases ⟶

Level of managerial demand decreases ⟶

Check ⟶ The manager plans a regular, scheduled meeting, update or report on or about the progress of the employee, team or team representative or supplier (etc.)

Check ⟵ The employee, or person who is in receipt of the delegated work, arranges the meeting and is responsible for producing and distributing details of own (team) performance

Report ⟵ Measures of performance are so clear and agreed that the employee reports by exception only, when performance falls outside of agreed limits or parameters

Figure 12.2 Check, check, report

be required) and a plan to recover from any wayward situation. If the worst or something less severe does happen, and it probably will, maybe not immediately, as a level of confidence or security (but hopefully not complacency) kicks in, it is essential to have pre-empted this, for a number of reasons. The first is that a drop in the operational standard or customer service level norm is a disadvantage to the business, which needs to be addressed immediately and the damage limited. The second is so that you as a manager are able to handle the situation, and not panic as a result, or worse, in my opinion, lose your faith in delegation as a means to success. The third, but arguably most important, is a plan, and a sense of reassurance that things can quickly get back on track means that you can be *supportive* to the person or team who you have delegated to.

Remember to remember that they could quite likely be distressed or stressed or certainly unsettled by the situation, too, and it is important to involve them in the solution and handling of the situation as the team proceeds to correct it. Naturally, there will be an element of proving that actions (or inactions/omissions or errors) have consequences, but this also has to be balanced with damage limitation.

Deliberately, I have played here to the worried and the concerned, so let this be said because it is as important, if not more important, than all the pre-emptive, preventative planning that one, as a delegating leader, can come up with. It's simple, oft forgotten and it goes like this:

Always remember to say thank you for the things that went well or even just as planned. Take time to add why you are so pleased. Hopefully, you would always thank a driver who let you out of the junction or a person who held the door open for you or the waiter who served you dinner etc. They are just doing their job (not open to a discussion about tipping protocols here), but there is no reason why you wouldn't say thank you, and actually it is right that you do. Same applies in the office and in business. Yes, you're doing what you are paid to do, but a thank you, or at least an acknowledgement, goes an extremely long way.[1]

---

[1] I refer here for support to Dr Julian Barling, who writes and researches impeccably on the science of management. My love for what he stands for, however, came when he simply stated that in spite of all the academic analysis around leadership the most charismatic leaders, or at least those that are most remembered as the most charismatic, are often those who simply remember names, say thank you often, acknowledge their own mistakes (i.e. apologize) and are clear about why they are grateful when they claim to be.

As things progress or get more comfortable, one could hopefully move to the next type of 'check' in the feedback process, the one where the delegated to are responsible for initiating the agreed and regular feedback, be it meeting or report. It is not the manager who has to fret about ensuring it is in the diary. The team member recognizes that he or she needs to give the reassurance rather than the manager take it. The meeting may be much the same, in truth – the agenda largely unchanged – but the psychological contract is developing and the employee is keen and confident to give all the positive feedback necessary to the manager to know that delegation was the right thing and all is met: work is being done as per the expectation, within budget and timescales and to the expected standards. Naturally, on occasion this may not be the case, but if the employee is the initiator then they would reasonably be expected to have their own plan B or potential solution to the problem or, if not, be a comfort with seeking advice as appropriate.

At the 'report' stage, things have progressed to an ideal scenario. Things are reported to the delegator *by exception* (i.e. when they have fallen outside of agreed parameters). Let's see this as the equivalent of a patient arranging to see a GP because something is not quite right. This is utopia in a delegation sense: you have made it. At this point feel free to visualize a holiday with no interruptions because everything is going well back at base. Congratulations.

Delegation case study scenarios

It is important to remember that delegation is a habit and, like any habit or routine, there will be times when it varies.

Just think exercise: we rarely keep it consistent but have measures which prompt us at least to think about it if not ensure we return to it (weight, shape, well-being etc.). Delegation is much the same, and as leaders we have to remind ourselves not to fall into delegation traps where work starts to come back to us or the team, or company performance starts to fall away. There are no hard-and-fast rules, but if delegation is like a muscle then there certainly exists an element of 'muscle memory' when one starts to reconnect with it properly.

Below are some sample and very outline scenarios of how delegation issues can present and how they might be remedied.

Symptom	Scenario	Issues	Remedy
New Leader Burnout	Manager promoted above peer group	Team resent being delegated to, manager doing everything to avoid confrontation and bad feeling	Open communication, clarity on the team 'why' and reaffirmation/reallocation of 'who' does 'what' Then ensure clear processes
Threat of over-shine	Demotivated micro-manager	Team bored and frustrated and under-empowered,	Manager to look at team 'why' in the broader context of organizational goals and create

(Continued)

Symptom	Scenario	Issues	Remedy
		manager not stretched	new interest/ responsibilities and stretch Reignites *need* to delegate
Guilty of absence	Manager out of office or absent to suit family com- mitments/ flexible working, for example	Team 'wonder' what manager does, feel undervalued, manager wracked with guilt as not 'doing' with team Common in 'long day' cultures	Reconnect with team 'why' and 'what' manager and members are each required to achieve Communicate and congratulate each other regularly
Double- sided sticky tape	Senior exec struggling to step up and let go of team duties	Exec has much to learn but feels dragged back into day-to-day by over-demanding team Losing confidence, feeling out of depth	Communicate team 'why' and agree how to get best from each other ('what'/'who'), encourage stretch Exec to review/ understand delegation process and apply *upwards* as well as downwards

Here is the cautionary note: you are still accountable, as a human, and you have in all probability delegated responsibility to a or some humans. So my advice is still to have a structured form of check for yourself to make sure all is well. It is well worth creating an audit process of sorts, just to be sure that no news really does mean good news and not a hidden collection of minor disasters waiting to explode. For me, I have an operational checklist that will forever form the structure of even the most casual updates:

- People: Do we have the right ones doing the right things well? If some are being carried, the carriers will eventually look to leave and the carried will be all that remain.

- Systems: Sadly, our dependence on technology means it has to be as good as possible in an otherwise uncertain world. Make sure the team has excellent support and training and a budget to accommodate.

- Processes: As we work through this checklist, the importance grows. You can only be certain of the resilience of the business if you know the team are doing what you expect; otherwise, even the managers you delegate to are trying to manage shifting sands. Process, adherence to it or agreed and documented movement away from it are vital.

- Performance: Performance measurement comes under three banners: standards (quality assurance, or QA), management information (key performance indicators, or KPIs) and financial (namely cash). Have ways to know all three are in great shape and being achieved.

My message here is that delegation is deep and it should be when done well, but it is not absolute (that would equate to 'dumping').

To further the medical analogy, having one's finger on the pulse does not mean hanging onto the patient's wrist at all times. One can take a pulse periodically and gain the results for oneself, in addition to listening to the testimony of the patient.

In short, don't assume all is well; be sure to ask the question one way or another. And when things are good, say so, loud and clear. It helps to ensure that teams know what good looks like. When things are less good, ask lots of questions. Find out why. Have they been left alone too long? Has there been a move away from procedure or protocol? If the answer to all is no then count your blessings: you're in an iterative stage of learning, briefing and delegation, and things can only get better as long as there is focus on continually deepening and improving the understanding of the process.

The Gift of Time is accompanied by an online programme that offers practical help, activities and accountability for action.[2]

---

[2]For more information go to http://thegiftoftime.yourgoalstoday.com/.

Part Four
DELEGATION IN CONTEXT

13
DELEGATION AS A NEW LEADER

I n management theory it is often cited as an essential skill yet often appears as a particularly lowly skill that almost comes naturally to new managers without much education or development. Of course, telling someone else what to do doesn't always have to happen in teams where tasks and roles are established and clear. It is probable that a team member promoted to 'run' the team doesn't actually have to delegate much at all, because everyone knows their roles and the status quo is maintained. The art and skill within delegation comes into play in this scenario when change is required or the dynamics change in some way. This may be because a team member leaves or a new team member joins, or costs are restricted and new pressures or systems arise.

Often such circumstances become the seedbed of poor delegation, because the manager has never had to delegate anew and suddenly there is a requirement to do so. Inexperience can mean that things go badly, relationships and performances are strained and all manner of consequences result. Delegation often reduces or even stops altogether, because the manager loses confidence in his or her ability to delegate well, and trust in the team or team member is damaged. In addition, attempted delegation becomes more stressful, often because it becomes resented by the team. In turn, morale can be affected and often is only improved because the manager takes up workload to assuage ill feeling and absorbs, or attempts to absorb, the strain, or avoids delegating altogether. Outcomes in these situations obviously vary and aren't guaranteed, but a manager who resents the perceived reluctance of their team to accept delegated tasks or responsibility is one who is often overqualified for their workload and naturally at risk of burnout, de-motivation, leaving the company and underperformance.

I believe this is because it is simply something that has to come quickly (one way or another, successfully and motivational or not) to an early manager. They simply have to get on with it. Rarely does responsibility come with appropriate training (ask your average super-hero) and so, in practical terms, the same applies to delegation.

If you're an established manager, that is to say you have been managing people for some time and do not regard yourself as a first-timer, you are probably reading this book because what it says applies to you: your early training did not cover how to successfully delegate sufficiently and thoroughly enough (if at all) to feel right about it now.

To that end I felt it appropriate to bring in the views of another guest expert – Gillian Davis, co-author of acclaimed international title *The First-Time Leader: Foundational tools to inspire and enable your new team*, whose work recognizes the unique situation that first-time managers find themselves in and assists them in building their skillset and finding their feet as they establish themselves as managers of people and progress towards their transformation into leaders of people. She has some sage advice to new leaders on the art of delegation and it is with pleasure and thanks that I hand over to her.

The best executive is one who has sense enough to pick good people to do what he wants done, and self-restraint enough to keep from meddling with them while they do it.

Theodore Roosevelt

When I started my first managerial role, I was overwhelmed with my new level of responsibility, as I had just started managing a team of eight, all of whom were a generation older than me. It was the first time I had this kind of responsibility, there was so much at stake and I felt like I had something to prove. Unsure how to handle it, I went into action without thinking. I started managing meetings like a drill sergeant. I spent a lot of time drawing up long strategy plans, worked all day, and most nights, and hardly ever delegated.

I was aware that this was one of my weak points, so I did attempt to delegate. I remember my mentor coming in after a team meeting, and I proudly showed him my task list (after I had delegated some work to my team).

He asked: 'What's all the highlighted yellow?'

'The yellow is my tasks; the green is what I delegated,' I replied, feeling very proud of myself.

'There is far too much yellow,' he responded.

It was then and there that I realized I had no idea how or what to delegate. As a first-time manager, it was very difficult to come to terms with the fact that it was no longer my responsibility to *do* the work but to ensure it *got done* by others.

Delegating was one of my biggest challenges but it got easier. It first became easier when I started recognizing common first-time leader mistakes, and traps. You've probably heard the saying 'Know your strengths and delegate your weaknesses', well, I took that on board and started figuring out what my strengths were. It has worked very well for me, and I hope I leave you with some easy ways to help you decide what to, and what not to, delegate.

It can be so easy to fall into common management traps when we don't take the time to figure out what our leadership style is. Often, we jump into the challenge head first, with the best of intentions, without seeking to understand why we are there.

Common first-time traps usually look something like this:

- **Controlling:** When we don't take the time to know ourselves, or our teams, we can't seem to let go of the work. I would say this is probably the biggest first-time leader mistake, and the most harmful one over time. When we control, we don't delegate and most importantly we don't inspire. We stifle creativity, therefore driving out talented and driven team members who will look for happiness elsewhere. It's also harmful to you. Being controlling is extremely stressful. You carry the weight of all the work on your shoulders. Instead of transferring what you want done, you do it yourself. This can lead to burnouts, projects failing because they can't be sustained by one person and disappointing a lot of important people.

- **Being busy, but not efficient:** When we don't delegate, and we end up carrying all the work we were doing in our previous role *and* trying to live up to the new set of expectations in our new role, we end up with way too much. Being busy and being efficient are two different things. Efficient people use time and skills accordingly. Busy people are always busy, and hardly produce good outputs. Being busy doesn't mean we're being productive. Have you ever had a manager whose most common response was, 'I'm too busy . . .'? How did that make you feel? Don't become that manager. Delegate so you have time and headspace to properly support your team.

- **Not innovating:** Managers become leaders when they start innovating. When you don't delegate, and you are too busy, you are managing. Too often, we fall into that trap, sometimes without even realizing it. Your role as a leader is to innovate, and you can only have clarity when you have the appropriate mental space to do so. That is made possible by effective delegation.

- **Stagnating team:** Your team is and will be your biggest ally. Your role as a leader is to ensure you can support and inspire them to make great things happen. When you don't delegate, you're not growing the skills in your team. It's important for you to shift your focus. As a leader, your job is to ensure that your objectives are reached by supporting your team to make it happen. You have to let go and delegate to be an effective leader. It's not up to you to physically do the work any more; you need that time to help others learn how to do it. A stagnating team is a leader's worst nightmare. It's hard to bring people back when they lose interest, don't feel valued or feel like they aren't growing. Your highest achievers will go to your competition. Don't allow that to happen!

So how do we avoid these common management traps and ensure we effectively delegate? When I co-wrote *First Time Leader: Foundational tools to inspire and enable your new team*, I was still working full-time. It became imperative to delegate my work in order to get it all done within the timelines the publisher had given us. Finding the support both at work and at home allowed me to complete one of my greatest achievements to date.

I first made a decision tree that looked something like Figure 13.1:

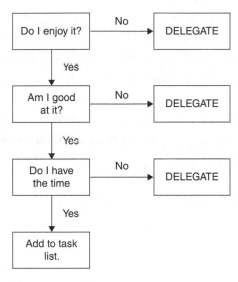

Figure 13.1 Decision tree.

Simple, I know, it but was very effective. As a people pleaser, my default answer to a question was to say 'Yes.' This tree allowed me to pause and see if it was something I should act on. I would add one more check box, however, and that would be 'Is it in line with my purpose/objective/goal?' If it isn't, it shouldn't be done. Stay on the path, and ensure that your goals and visions are crystal clear.

To get a better understanding of what you should do, and what and how to delegate, we will run through six steps to delegation that I outline in *First Time Leader.*

Step 1: Do what you love and what you can do well.

When I work with first-time managers, the first thing I have them do is write down all the tasks they, and their team, are responsible for. We then go through and highlight all the tasks that they enjoy (doesn't matter if it's admin, or highly strategic). Doing what you love makes you happy, and gives you good energy. Energy that you, and others around you, can vibe off. When you do things you hate, they usually drain you of good energy, and therefore take you away from the things that make you happy. Always do what you love!

Step 2: Do what you have to get done.

Some things you just have to get done. Maybe it's to make the customer happy, your boss happy, your team happy, etc. Whatever it is, these are things you can't delegate. You are physically and mentally capable of doing these tasks, but they don't get you out of bed in the morning. To make sure these tasks don't get the best of you, especially if you don't enjoy them, allocate a certain time per week that you dedicate to these tasks. This will ensure these tasks don't take over the majority of your time, and take you away from tasks that you love, or are exceptional at. If you really feel these tasks are not a good fit for you, but at the moment, can't delegate, start taking notes as to who would be the best person in your team to train so that you are able to delegate it. For the meantime, whatever it is that you're doing, give it that 100% effort it deserves.

Step 3: Just delegate.

When you know your team well, you know what their capabilities and strengths are. This allows for some pretty seamless delegation. When you have all the tasks written out, it's easy to start matching specific tasks to specific people. It's helpful to have a team grid handy to remind yourself whose strengths fall where, so when you are faced with a task, you can immediately match it to the right person. Like Step 1, you should try when you can to match tasks to your team members' individual strengths so that they are also doing what they love.

Step 4: Delegate and support.

When you can't delegate to someone's strengths, you have to be mindful that this person will require extra time and support. For example, finances and analytics are not my strength; however, my boss only spoke numbers. It was a challenge for me to put together an effective, detail-oriented business plan. I had one of my detail-oriented team members support me in writing a business plan, and it was amazing to see how quickly my projects started to get approved. On the flip side, when I had a presentation to delegate, or something more creative, and I had to delegate that to my detail-oriented team member because of lack of resources, I knew I had to give them more time, support and encouragement as I was taking them out of their comfort zone. It's so important to understand your team to be better able to delegate and the best way to do this is to ask them.

Step 5: Do later.

Sometimes it can feel like everything is important, and everything needs to get done NOW or else you'll be disappointing a lot of people who need those things to be done.

By being focused and clear on what *you* need to achieve to get to where you want to go, you should be clear on what your priorities are. Priorities always go to the top of the pile. Things that still need to get done but are not one of your priorities can go in the 'do later' pile, but make sure you manage the expectations of those waiting for it. Being realistic with your timelines to others shifts the accountability to those who are waiting for the completion of the task. If they aren't satisfied with the time it will take to have it done, they can choose to send the task to someone else. Get comfortable in this place, get comfortable not being the 'go to' person for everything and don't see someone taking something off you as a bad thing. People respect your time when you start to respect it yourself.

Step 6: Don't do.

Following on from Step 5, get comfortable saying 'No' to tasks that are not important to you and your team objectives. In your position as leader, you may find that the amount of inquiries and demands of your time will start to increase. Whether it's bringing you into a meeting, inviting you to an event, asking for an interview or asking for lunch, saying yes to all these invites can take you away from what's most important. Ensure that you and your team are getting done what needs to be done to satisfy your most important stakeholder, ensure that you are surrounded by people and tasks that give you positive energy, give yourself sufficient time to recharge your batteries and say no to anything that will drain you and take you away from what's important and not in line with your goals.

Delegation: A constant WIP

I don't believe delegating is something we keep getting better and better at. It will ebb and flow. Sometimes we can let life get the best of us and it's only then that we realize how off track we've become with our delegation abilities. Imagine that you are always a work in progress (WIP). Sometimes, you'll be on top of everything; other times you'll end up with too much on your plate. Putting the right steps in place to prevent you don't fall into the trap is what will help you along the way. Always be clear on what your strengths are, keep getting to know your team so you understand their strengths and weaknesses and keep your eye on the prize. Be focused on your objectives and goals, so you can delegate between what needs to get done, what can wait and what you can ignore. Don't try to be everything to everyone, as you'll end up being nothing to no one.

Delegating is a skill that first timers need to get comfortable with. Understand that to reach your goals, you cannot do it alone. The most successful business owners surround themselves with talented teams and enable and inspire them to move towards a common goal, together, as one. Your role and focus as a leader is to share what that big picture is, and ensure everyone is on the same path. Relieve the stress from your shoulders and invite your team to come with you on your journey.

Remember to enjoy the ride.

14
DELEGATION AND OTHER LEADERSHIP SKILLS

H ere we focus on delegation in the context of other leadership and management skills and examine where delegation fits in the management toolkit.

The reason why I focus so obsessively on delegation is because I so fundamentally believe that delegation is a fulcrum skill in the management toolkit.

You see, if you meet, know or get to work with someone who is acknowledged to be a good delegator then it is highly unlikely that they are lacking other leadership pre-requisites.[1] A good delegator will be a strategist with a formidable range of skills,

---

[1] By 'good delegator', I mean someone who themselves would agree that they delegate well and achieve the desired results they require from a happy and functional team. Equally, their team members and colleagues would agree that the leader is a comfortable and well-supported one, clear and (usually) unstressed (not to be confused with unpressured). If the leader has superiors or shareholders to whom they report or are accountable, it would generally be agreed that the leader receives their responsibilities and any new or additional projects or tasks well and comprehensively and delivers on requirements through the support of their team.

THE GIFT OF TIME

including leadership, planning, negotiation, communication as well as an astute commercial awareness.

The best productivity hack is delegation

Source: Published on LinkedIn by Frank Wu, Huff Post blogger, http://www.linkedin.com/today/post/article/20140121123851-13561052-productivity-hacks-the-alchemy-of-delegation?trk=prof-post, accessed 10th October 2010.

Everyone wants to do more by doing less. This notion is our modern-day alchemist's illusion. There are many means to improve incrementally. But there are few honest means to change significantly.

Giving work to other people has the greatest potential. That is the definition of delegation. Giving work to other people. It also is among the most difficult, exasperating, seemingly futile aspects of management.

Here are six tips for leaders who wish to delegate well. A prefatory note to my colleagues: I am self-aware enough to realize I, too, fail in every regard noted here. I have compiled these suggestions for myself as much as for others.

First, the point is 'giving work to other people.' It is not dumping YOUR work on OTHER people. It's giving them work that they come to own.

The people who report to you must see that you are putting in as much effort as you are asking of them. If you truly are that much more efficient than others are then you are obliged to set a higher expectation of productivity for yourself, for the sake of sustained goodwill and good morale.

Second, probably the most demanding aspect of delegating is in fact doing it. Successful people have achieved their supervisory roles by performing in a superlative manner, with a few exceptions that cannot last. That means they tend to believe, not utterly without reason, that they could execute a project better than the person to whom they might assign it. You cannot proceed further unless you disabuse yourself of this conceit — the more you believe it, the more likely you are wrong.

If you cannot accept outcomes that are different than what you would have achieved for yourself, including results that are minimally acceptable by your standards, you should not try this technique. You will set up a self-fulfilling prophecy with your temptation to interfere, frustrating everyone until you meet your own deserved demise as a supervisor.

Third, your instructions need to be clear. Almost all of us have this concept down, except backwards. It doesn't matter what you said. It matters what they heard. Even if your thoughts are set down in writing, it's your own fault if they are misunderstood. You have to see the world from someone else's perspective. A command creates resentment anywhere outside the military.

In the cult classic movie *Monty Python's Quest for the Holy Grail*, there is the scene in which the father of the groom gives orders to the guards to watch the reluctant young man before his nuptials. He is flummoxed by the dimwittedness of his servants, and there could be no better example of the normal course of affairs whether in English comedy or contemporary business. The extended series of misunderstandings is worth watching. It is not atypical.

Fourth, you have to hire well. I learn from my mistakes. My most serious errors have been about people, not ideas. People are, well, human. They are complex. Every member of your team needs to function at the highest level of competence. It is as clichéd as it is true.

Fifth, everything else depends on trust. As much as individuals are complex, groups of people are even more complex. Relationships are paramount. You are compelled to cultivate your teammates, which you should be doing anyway aside from any desire to delegate.

Sixth, know what cannot be delegated. The rule is this: Credit to them, blame to you. It is your name, your reputation and your career at stake, without pause. So it must be your judgment call, with all the risks associated with any decision. The content belongs to you, with the customary author's note about who owns the errors. Coordination and conflict resolution also must be taken care, from the top.

There you have it. Delegate, delegate, delegate.

15
DISASTROUS DELEGATION

I will now use an episode of my own experience as a case study for disastrous delegation.

What's important here is that nothing that follows reflects on anyone else's skills, intentions or ability, except my own. It is also fairly extreme, though hopefully that helps to make the point.

A business I launched had been established less than two years when I gave birth to my first child. I had no maternity leave for the first and little more for the second some 17 months later. Nonetheless, I had been pretty good at delegating and a manager was employed to run the operation and team.

After five years I had opened another new business (actually my fourth), in retail this time, and the running of the first business in question was largely delegated. It certainly ran at a distance, as I was remote from it by hundreds of miles, with a growing team and growing profitability.

As the first business appeared to thrive, the newer one faced an imploding economy, huge hikes in costs through fuel and food price increases and some of the worst weather the century had seen. As it was a high-end, food-based, quality-led product located in a tourist area, none of this was good news. The first business supported the second financially while I hoped to steer the thing through to better times. Big mistake in itself, as it happens, but that's another story and it's not relevant to the learning with regard to my disastrous delegation.

In my haste to delegate managerial responsibility for the first business I had compromised in my recruitment, taking what was available at the time rather than looking objectively at what the business needed. I did not take the time to find the most suitable 'who'. The business was nonetheless well run, gave a great service to its clients and, as I said, was profitable, but in not reviewing what had been delegated I missed a number of tricks and in the end had to divest my other businesses to return and rescue the first business from administration. Extreme, I know, and it took some three years to get back on track with everything returned to its glory days of process (and systems), communication and delegation coming together successfully. I refer you here to the Delegation Venn diagram and the letters 'w', 'p' and 'e' on it. Naturally, this was somewhat hampered by recession and economic downturn but in truth it was a good business, with a solid footing and good business model, in a market sector that was only set to grow – and always grows through harder times. So what went wrong?

I have said elsewhere, and it is well known, that a disaster never really results from one single thing going wrong, even though

that's how it may appear on the surface. A disaster is the cul-
mination of a number of small things all going wrong, if not at
once then in quick succession before each individual situation
can be remedied or recovered. It doesn't have to be very many
either, as little as three can do the trick.[1]

In the first instance (get ready, I will run the gamut here), everything started so very well. Unexpected and unplanned change
of management resulted in a panic appointment of an employee
who had previously been rejected (time). As a result of this, delegation was extreme and badly planned, leaving the situation in
one of extreme 'w'. The job was to manage a team doing the day-
to-day without their really knowing or being highly cognizant of
the true client motivation. Not really understanding *why* people
buy from us as well as why people would want to was because it
had not been communicated properly and repeatedly – by me.
I understood it, of course, but the team only really saw it from
their side. The most crucial 'why', though, was why I had delegated the business itself to be run without me. I utterly moved
away from getting this across through my day-to-day relationship with the business and in doing so failed hugely in communicating the 'why' my delegation of the operation was relevant
to us all.

---

[1] On the upside here, it is useful to bear in mind that its converse is stellar success!
That is to say, major success is usually the result of a number of positive instances
falling in line at the same time or within a short time of each where the cumulative
benefits add up to, for example, a product or service that is of relevance in its
function, of the moment in its awareness, commercially acceptable in its pricing
and attractive in its fashion or vogue.

Lack of communication about the team's importance to the success of the business, as well as a lack of structured feedback mechanisms, then resulted in the pristinely documented and clear processes that had been put together to run the business being bypassed, circumvented and to a greater degree ignored ('p'). During this phase of procedural discipline, time wasn't taken to ensure all the groundwork that had been put into SOPs (standard operating procedures) was understood and retained in practice. In addition, because it was critical to get a person in the seat quickly, we compromised over the replacement's required skillset. That's my business right there, firmly rooted at this point in area 'p'.

Ironically, the status moved to 'e' pretty quickly. When I returned to resume the helm and effectively to ultimately undo a decade of steadiness as opposed to aggressive growth, what I found was a team clear that they were delegated to (and you can read for that 'on their own' in spite of considerable amounts of my time spent apparently guiding them through and coaching them on, but not acting on, the management information that resulted), but they were sticking to ineffective operational methods that had grown organically and without structure away from the original procedures. This may sound oxymoronic but in truth they were not empowered to see things in any other way. This was essentially how things had allegedly 'always been done', although the link to the original intention was slipping all the time and the feeling of lack of empowerment had resulted in a status quo that could have been terminal to the business.

Putting things back together meant (it hurts to say) retrieving the empowerment operationally (or undoing the delegation in order to straighten everything out operationally), then re-gifting it to the team. Throughout, this included their input into process creation and contribution to strategy through communication. In effect, entirely new systems, with new operations procedures (driven by me but created collectively) were needed. Not much short of starting the business again with a significant team refreshment. High levels of communication, coupled with a dose of humility and vulnerability on my part, were needed to re-empower the team and delegate the business again. Operational, system and process stability re-positioned their responsibilities back into the right place: to innovate, create, develop and grow the business from a position of firm foundations.

16
DELEGATION FOR PARENTS

Oh my, there's heaps to say on this one, and Elizabeth O'Shea – a most revered parental coach regularly called upon by the BBC and Sky for her comments and expertise in parenting issues – contributes a most insightful chapter on parenthood and delegation. Her central thesis got me straightaway: 'Our job as a parent is to make ourselves redundant.'

After all, redundancy is the ultimate delegation. Who'd have thought that something so thoroughly aligned with the negative could ultimately become so positive?

I have defined four types of delegation: downwards, upwards, sideways and silent. At home, the latter two are the only ones in my opinion that should exist. As a child of the seventies, Dad thought he was boss, Mum knew she was and we/I were most definitely subordinates. As a parent of teens, rank seems to diminish to nothing. Kids know their rights and exercise them with aplomb. Those stalwart phrases that silenced us so thoroughly – 'Because I told you so' and 'Do as you're told' – mean nothing today and that 'Children should be seen and not heard' resonates only, we hope, with the Victorian age. Of course, this is a good thing, but the new generation of parents dealing with their children as equals are still required to hand over the skills of life and ensure they are well equipped as young adults, ready to face the world. Given this new found 'equality', parents are obviously finding it ever harder to delegate to their children, our constant involvement in their lives – tending to their needs as opposed to letting them fend for themselves – makes it harder to strike the balance of nurture and 'love' versus independence.

My children say regularly to each other, 'Why do I have to do that?' and the other will answer, 'Because she's big into delegation, remember?' It's true, of course, and my/our position as parents with them is clear. If it is something they are old enough to do for themselves, they ought to do it for themselves, and if they don't have to because we choose to do it for them, it is because it is a gift from us, and not a right of theirs.

Sounds strict? Yes, I think it is, but I *know* that I can pack their school backpack or weekend bag, do their homework (I think!), make a cheese sandwich or iron a t-shirt and I don't feel it necessary to prove that to anyone, least of all them. It's not a competition for me. I'm not up for the 'mother stakes' insofar as ensuring that all is in order, because I have run myself ragged while everyone else watched the nearest screen, just so I can prove I am a 'good mum'. I have been hugely inspired by the Cub Scout organisation. From an early age our boys have camped and slept over at Cub events and been encouraged by Akela to pack their own bag, so *they know what they have got*, where it is and what they need to take home with them at the end. It also means that they can't 'blame mum for forgetting'.

It takes some courage to be this kind of parent and one does occasionally feel judged somehow. But the sense of pride we all have when one of our boys has cooked us all a meal, changed the bed covers or just helped to unload the groceries is immense. They are on their way to independence and they are enjoying the journey, rather than being nagged at a later age for taking everything for granted and contributing nothing.

Actions and consequences have always been essential parts of their childhood in all aspects of their upbringing. If they forget it, they can't use it; if they spend it, they can't save it. Conversely, if they do it, they are self-sufficient. They order from the menu for themselves and have done from an early age. They take their own pocket money to the counter and feel the pride of buying their own treats. I think it gives them confidence and accountability and it requires some will to keep it up, because it's often so much easier just to give in and do it for them.

The experts in this book have all had free rein to write from their own perspectives on delegation with no brief from me other than my delegation pathway and belief in its inherent value and largely underrated capacity to produce many good things. When Elizabeth asked me what I wanted her to write, I simply said whatever you think about delegating to children. She then asked, given my purported expertise in delegation, why I didn't just do it for myself. Great question. Then I felt my face crumple and my parental angst kick in and that threw up only one answer: when it comes to parenting, I confess I simply don't feel qualified. I do what I think is right, 100% out of love and then hope for the best. I was so pleased and not a little relieved, therefore, when I saw what she came up with.

Elizabeth O'Shea is one of the UK's leading parenting experts. She has four children of her own and over 20 years' parenting experience. She appears regularly on BBC radio, including Radio 4's *Woman's Hour* – and TV and Sky News, helping parents solve their parenting issues. Ten thousand parents visit her website each month, looking for advice for dealing with their children. Let her talk to you now about common ground we didn't know we had until we started sharing tales of our children: a passion for the strategic inclusion, and importance, of delegation in the parental toolkit.

The most important thing that parents can teach their children is how to get along without them.

Frank Clark

The day my children started primary school aged four, they were magically able to wipe their own bottoms and make their own lunchboxes. And the day they started secondary school aged eleven they were suddenly able to manage all their own homework and assignments!

Elizabeth O'Shea

Just as delegation can make your time at work easier, it can also help to make life at home happier and more manageable. Any child over the age of three can do jobs at home and become more independent so you don't have to do so much for them or clean up after them. If you're thinking that there is no way you can train a child to help at three years old, just remember how you potty trained your child. When you knew you needed to get your child out of nappies, persistence and creativity were key to successfully training your child to use the toilet. And both of those skills will be useful if you would like to share the workload, and encourage your child (and partner?) to help at home.

Benefits of delegating to your children

The benefits of delegating to your children are that they can become more self-reliant, more independent and help around the house, freeing up more of your time. You can spend more quality time with your child, without feeling stressed and hassled about the volume of work at home. You can feel confident that your child is able to do things for themselves and it takes the pressure of feeling you have to do everything for your child away. Sometimes parents can feel resentful that they do so much for their children – without appreciation or gratitude. Delegating to your child can help your son or daughter do things *for* you rather than expecting all the jobs at home to be done *by* you.

The benefits to your child are that they get the confidence that they can do things for themselves. They learn life skills that will prepare them for adulthood, and they'll begin to appreciate what you do for them when they understand what's involved in all the tasks you do. And a big benefit is that when they start contributing and helping there will be less moaning and nagging going on at home, making it a more pleasant place to be for everyone.

An interesting added bonus is that children who help at home and do more for themselves are less likely to be bullied. Children who take on responsibilities at home feel more empowered and confident. They are also less likely to engage in premature sex, smoke cigarettes, rely on alcohol or take drugs. So in the long run you may be helping your child more than you imagined by getting them to help around the house!

Why don't we delegate to our children sooner?

So why don't we teach our children to be self-reliant sooner? Initially, it may be because of the time it takes to teach our children how to help. Some parents don't know how to motivate their children. Often, parents hate to see their children grumpy or struggling and would rather do the job themselves than deal with a child's reluctance to help. Some parents may be worried that their child will hurt themselves or may think that it's just easier and quicker to do it themselves. Or they may have no confidence that their child will do a good job. Or perhaps they do everything themselves out of habit because they've always done it.

And there are some deeper underlying issues that keep parents doing everything for their children. It gives parents a role. Many parents equate doing things for their children as proof of their love. They show their affection by doing things for their child. This is particularly true if a child has had to cope with hardships or difficulties growing up, such as a divorce or illness, and parents want to make their life a little easier.

And doing everything gives parents a sense that they're in control. It's hard to let go of tasks that may not be done as quickly and efficiently as they could do themselves! Also, when parents do all the tasks at home, everybody in the house depends on them. And that's a nice feeling – to be needed. Letting go can be hard because it stops parents being the central sun around which all the planets revolve.

Here's a sobering thought, however...

In no society in the world are slaves respected!

When you wash and cook and shop and clean for your child, they come to expect it. You may think your child is selfish or spoiled, but in actual fact you have trained him or her to expect you to do everything for them. In fact, you may even think that's your job.

Just imagine for a moment that you employed a cleaner for your home. And one day, after many years your cleaner came up to you and said.

'I've had enough! You expect me to do all the cleaning around here. Well, it's about time you started to help. Can you get up off the sofa and start clearing the mess up in here and then come and help me in the kitchen?'

THE GIFT OF TIME

What would you think? You'd probably be surprised. But because she's been with you for many years you may think she had forgotten her place. Perhaps you may decide to do what she asks but secretly wonder what on earth has got into her.

If you suggest to your child, after years of clearing up after them, they should start helping out, they'll be surprised and confused. They'll think it's your job. They may decide that for an easy life it may be better to do what you ask. But they won't put their heart into it. And secretly they'll be plotting to do as little as possible and hope that you remember your role is to look after them! In truth, your child thinks that clearing and cleaning and shopping and cooking are your job. Because that's the way it's always worked in your house. Why should they be grateful for you doing your job?

However, it's your role as a parent to raise your child to be a responsible adult who can care for themselves with all the life skills they need. So how can you delegate more, change your child's view towards believing that being part of a family means working together and get them to take on regular jobs or chores?

Your job as a parent is to make yourself redundant.

When you remember that, you realise the importance of encouraging your child to do things for themselves and help round the house – and to increase your expectations as they grow older. If your child leaves home not being able to clean, wash their clothes, cook and clear up after themselves, they'll struggle, and you won't have done your job preparing them for the outside world. Just think how well your child would get on with their future flatmates or partner if they can't even clear up after themselves.

If you overprotect your child and do too much for them, you'll set them up to be demanding and unpopular. If you don't train them to do things for themselves, your child will learn how to be helpless. They won't learn to trust their own abilities or judgements. They'll expect everything to be done for them and they won't appreciate what *is* done for them – so they'll become spoilt. They won't develop basic skills that they'll need. They won't learn how to persevere at things and so they'll have a low self-esteem. And they won't become nice people to live with because they'll grow up with an air of expectation that other people are there to do things for them.

Most parents would say that they want their children to be happy. If we just focus on making children happy, it's easy to confuse what children want with what they need. In order to have happy, productive, successful and meaningful lives, children need to know how to be independent, to rely on themselves and have all the skills when they leave home to be fully-functioning adults. The earlier you start, the earlier it is to pass the skills on to your child. Because, in the early years, children think adults' work is fun. That's why they make 'working' toy ovens and vacuum cleaners! In the words of Mary

Poppins – 'In every job that's to be done there is an element of fun. You find it and – snap! – the job's a game!'

What to do with the time you save when you delegate

Your family and your children are the most important people in the world to you. Your children can provide so much pleasure and fun, and bring out your relaxed, happy, playful nature. And when they're old enough to leave home you will be delighted every time they make plans to come back to visit you. You probably want to have such a really close bond with your children that they want to visit you often.

If you use the time that you save when you delegate at home, to spend quality time with your children and family it will be really beneficial. Spending one-to-one time with each of your children, talking, playing, connecting and making the bond between you stronger and more loving, will make delegation at home a win–win for everyone. And you and your child will love the difference it creates in your home.

Being part of a family means everyone helps

It's important to explain to your child that being part of a family means everyone helps – that everyone supports each other and works together as a team. You can talk to them about why you're asking them to help – how it will help their self-esteem and confidence. And how much happier they'll be if they can do things independently. You can tell them that your job as a parent is to help them to be independent and care for themselves, and this is how you can help them do that. And you can explain that every child should do jobs around the house for free, because there are responsibilities as well as benefits to being in your family.

Help your child to be independent

It's also useful to think about what your child could be doing for themselves. You can use the same methods and techniques to teach your children to care for themselves, to be independent in washing and dressing. Able to get themselves up and ready in the morning, and ready for bed at night. Able to pack their own schoolbag and make their own lunch. Able to keep their belongings tidy and clear up after making a mess. And able to keep their things organized and plan how to get homework and tasks done. Once your child develops the habits of self-reliance, you will find a lot of your time is freed up. And life at home will be much less stressed.

What jobs could your child do to help?

Sometimes it helps to think – if you could ask your child to do anything and you knew the answer would be 'yes' – what job would you ask your child to do? What would you love to delegate? What would you ask if you knew there wouldn't be a fuss?

Let's look at what children can do at different ages:

Toddlers and pre-school children, up to age 4, can:

- clear the table

- dust

- empty waste paper baskets

- lay the table

- put their toys away

- sort books and magazines

- sort out the recycling

- wipe surfaces.

Primary school children, aged 4 to 11, can:

- care for a pet or walk the dog

- change sheets

- clean kitchens and bathrooms

- dust, vacuum and wash up

- help make lunchboxes

- help make dinner

- help with grocery shopping

- keep bedroom tidy

- mop floors

- peel vegetables

- put away groceries

- rake leaves

- sweep floors

- take out bins

- tidy their own bedrooms

- unload and load the dishwasher

- wash skirting boards and white-painted woodwork

- wash table and side-counters after meals

- wash the car

- wash the dishes

- wash walls

- wash windows

- wash, dry and fold laundry and put clothes away

- water flowerbeds

- water indoor plants

- weed the garden.

Secondary school children, aged 11 to 18, (boys as well as girls) can:

- continue all of the above (including tidying up after themselves!)

- babysit for friends or relatives (if old enough)

- babysit younger siblings

- clean oven

- cook meals for the whole family

- do the grocery shopping

- help maintain the car

- iron clothes

- mend clothes

- mow the lawn

- sew buttons

- and I'm sure you'll be able to think of a few other jobs your child could do too!

Coaching skills

It's good if you can think of yourself as a coach for your child. Like a football coach, certain things will help your child feel more able to do new jobs or take over a new responsibility. If you want your child to learn new skills, how can you coach them? What skills do you need that will make your child happier to take on new responsibilities and do more for themselves?

First, always try to stay calm, patient, friendly and positive with your child. No one likes to be shouted at. So try to be motivating and happy. And if you find yourself getting annoyed or your child starts losing their temper, stop! You can always try again the following day.

It's good to listen to your child's difficulties and frustrations. It can be hard to learn a new skill – and even harder for your child to do it when they're tired or in a bad mood. Stick with it. They'll soon learn. And rather than telling them what to do it's useful to ask questions, so your child has to think about what they need to do. Keep asking relevant questions about what job they'll need to do when they get home, or how they'll remember what to pack in their schoolbag in the morning.

As your child becomes more independent, it's good if you can take a back seat when it comes to offering advice or trying to fix things for your child so they learn to think for themselves. To get them to solve any problems they have taking on new jobs, you can brainstorm ideas, solutions and strategies with them. And get them to choose which one they think will work best. If you can trust your child, they'll start to see themselves as capable and able to do things, and learn to live up to that trust.

When you're teaching your child, be clear and brief and give simple instructions. If you can, break the task down into small steps, so your child masters each little skill, then gradually help them put the steps together.

Children love a competition, so challenge your child to beat the timer or to remember each of the steps better than they did the previous week, so they feel motivated to keep trying to achieve the goal. And don't forget: timers are a great little aid to take the pressure off you, and have a set end time for an activity. For instance, a timer can tell your child when they have washed a floor for a full 10 minutes!

It's good to make sure that you have realistic expectations of what your child can do at their age. Just because it is listed above, doesn't necessarily mean your child is able to do it. Children develop at different rates, so choose jobs that are suitable for *your* child. And then let them know your expectations, what needs to be done and when so they can get into good habits.

In the early days, you can encourage and support your child by staying nearby, praising their efforts and keeping them focused on the goal. Empathize with their difficulties: when they don't want to do a job, let them know you're on their side. Give them lots of positive attention for their efforts, for the things they achieve, for not giving up, for not complaining and for being willing to learn.

Gradually you can experiment with different strategies and find what works. It may be that you do a job alongside your child for weeks and get them to copy you. Remember: time invested in teaching your child properly will be well rewarded with the time you'll save in the long run. Children hate to be rushed. If you see the time you put in as an investment, you will soon find that you reap the rewards. And life at home will be so much calmer and happier – for you as well as your child.

Don't forget to make learning the new jobs fun. Use humour and banter and 'in jokes' to make learning the new skill more fun. And make sure they know what the rewards are for a job well done.

How do you get your child to start helping?
Plan ahead

First, plan how you'll introduce the fact you want your child to help around the house in a way that explains the *benefits to them*. Think of yourself as a salesperson, selling something your child really needs but initially may be reluctant to accept!

Make a list of all the jobs you think your child *could* do. So they can choose what job or jobs they'd like to try or take on. This gives them some responsibility for taking on the job.

Work out what you feel would be fair for them to do, bearing in mind their age and ability. And remember to start gradually so that your child can learn one job first and then take on other jobs as they get older and more confident.

Make sure you set aside enough time to teach your child well, when neither of you is stressed or rushed, so you can enjoy doing the job together.

And plan to start when you can be sure you will stay positive and cheerful. An older child *may* be thinking that moaning, dragging their feet and doing a bad job will help you remember your place as the cleaner. So be prepared!

Show your child what to do

Teach them to do the job they've chosen. Use your coaching skills and explain how they do the job. Show them how you do it, while you talk aloud about what you're doing.

Do the task together

Then let them help you. Let them try each different step of the chore, until they feel confident. And gradually let them do more and more, then watch them doing each step. Coach them until they feel confident to do the job on their own. When you feel happy that your child knows how to do the job, check that they feel able to do it independently. If they don't, keep working alongside them until they feel confident. And remember to stay positive and friendly.

It's useful to ask how they'll judge whether they've done a good job. And let them know your expectations. So if you're showing them how to vacuum a room, a good job may mean there are no bits on the carpet and that there is no dust in the corners .

Watch them do it on their own

Then let them do it alone. And you just check that the job's been done well – check that they can do everything, and are safe and competent. And give them lots of detailed praise and positive attention.

Plan how they can keep up doing the job and remember to do it regularly

Your child needs to choose a regular time to do the job. Agree what time each day or week they'll do the job. If the job needs doing every day, like feeding a pet, check how they'll remember to do it. Alternatively, perhaps everyone in the family does the washing up and clearing up after each meal. Or could everyone help to clean the house on a Saturday morning?

Lastly, you need to hand over responsibility. The idea is that you don't have to nag and remind them to do the job. If they're likely to forget, keep asking questions to check when they'll do it and how they'll remember. So... on a Wednesday, what are you going to do? And how will you remember? And how will you know if you've done a good job? Remember that, to start with, they won't do the job as well as you could. However, bit by bit, they'll improve. Make it a habit to notice and comment when your child does a good job, or if they remember to do the job without your asking. And thank them with a smile and a hug. Let go of your perfectionism and enjoy the fact that you are getting help around the house.

If your child forgets or they don't do a good job, don't crit-icize them or nag them. Tell them what you expect and how they've fallen short of your expectation. Then simply ask them when they'll finish the job. A new habit takes 60 days to form, and there may be occasional days when your child really doesn't feel like helping, so be understanding but firm about what you expect. And keep emphasizing the benefits to them.

And finally

It's important to reward your child's efforts and plan some fun time with you – or as a family – to show that everyone

THE GIFT OF TIME

doing their bit to help results in more fun. Perhaps you could plan a small outing or time together as a family? Or perhaps share some time having a drink and a snack together after all the jobs are done? This shouldn't involve spending a lot of money. This isn't payment for them doing a job; it's the enjoyment of being able to spend more quality time together because you have more time if they help around the home. And to help them get the feel-good factor of being part of a family team.

And, lastly, try not to do things for your child that they're able to do for themselves. With each passing year, your child will become more capable, and will be able to do more and more. So remember *why* you're doing this. And try to help them learn the skills that will make them independent and able to go out into the world as capable young men and women.

CONCLUSION: TO ONLY DO, WHAT ONLY YOU CAN DO

I view this as the ultimate in delegation (split infinitive and all). I position it, however, as a quest and I believe the ability to get to this level of delegation and maintain it to the benefit of all is the province of the most successful in business.

The term itself is not my own. It was inspired by a friend of mine, then a finance director of a major corporation, who instinctively did the maths (no pun intended here) when it came to her own value and the insanity of overpaying her to do work that others could not only do, but also benefit from doing as part of their own career development.

If we only did what only we could do, i.e. if we focused on what we did best that differentiates us from our peers and our team, then we would be free to be our best in an unfettered way. The creativity that is needed for us to employ our skills to best effect requires time for our brains to think and focus. Case studies are a great way to illustrate this in action, though it can be rare to find.

This is an appropriate place for my own story to creep in as a case study. Since the beginning of 2014, I have been building everything towards only doing what only I can do.

It means saying no. It means going back to the delegation drawing board and starting again. It means re-connecting with delegation and all it entails to keep it right. It means that, although sometimes I am insanely busy (because I am my own worst enemy and keep getting involved in new projects), I genuinely spend much of my time doing what I love. Even though writing this book has been a challenge and a pressure, I have loved the whole thing. Delegation is not about necessarily having an easy life, kicking back and putting your feet up (unless that's your 'why', of course). I delegate a lot but I am still a busy person. I'm just a busy person working to my rules, with people I love working with, doing stuff I enjoy most. Not a bad gift to receive, is it?

The Gift of Time is accompanied by an online programme which offers practical help, activities and accountability for action.[1]

---

[1] For more information go to http://giftoftime.yourgoalstoday.com/.

APPENDIX 1: THE ART OF DELEGATION WHITE PAPER

D elegation at its most basic level is worth almost £300 billion per year to SMEs alone.

Gail Thomas

March 2013

This statistic simply cannot be ignored.

Vital time and therefore applied skill is wasted by business owners, managers and executives who continually perform tasks that they are overqualified to perform, inadequately and slowly, rather than delegate them to others who would welcome the work and challenge.

At the expense of business growth.

At the expense of employing others who would welcome delegated work.

We have to facilitate delegation through:

- education and training
- business opportunity
- new business start up
- business growth
- direct employment
- flexible employment
- the provision of reliable, cost-effective tangible alternatives
- funded assistance
- government support and initiatives.

We have to facilitate delegation. It is simply too valuable to ignore.

Background

In the summer of 2012, Vince Cable made a statement (an impossible and unattainable one but a powerful one nonetheless). He said, and I paraphrase, that there are 4.8 million SMEs in the UK today and if we had 900 000 more tomorrow we wouldn't have an economic problem. Those extra businesses would mean sufficient contribution that there would be acceptable level of deficit, the pension pot for the future would be sorted and unemployment would be reduced.

The 24-hour period required already renders the above impossible, in addition current ad hoc stats for the success rates of start-ups mean that somewhere in the region of 90 million new businesses would be required to ensure the survival of a mere 900 000.

But as I sat in the audience I did the maths and remained undaunted by the thought. Nine hundred thousand is 19% of 4.8 million. So presumably, if the businesses that already exist could grow by 19%, the net effect would be the same? If we remove the impossible 24-hour timescale, surely the growth would still be welcome and, to my mind, so achievable.

If we added 900 000 new businesses to the £4.8 million we already have – tomorrow, we wouldn't have an economic problem.

Premise

So what enables businesses to grow? Money, apparently, for one, but the banks aren't lending and any investment available is more gained from owners and shareholders and directed towards working capital and survival than development, employment and growth.

Hard times require greater creativity, to create new methods of marketing, new products, improvement in process and strategic reassessment. This requires time. If time is a commodity that frees up resources that, when freed up, enable growth through creativity, time needs to be freed up easily and cost-effectively within SMEs (and corporates, NGOs, charities and government organizations).

Would time – freed up – enable business growth?

Anecdotal support

The light-bulb moment came when I realized that a business I set up over a decade ago helped businesses to grow through the art of delegation. I set it up because I needed some secretarial support and call answering and I still use it as a client today to free up my time so I can be a mum as well as a businessperson.

I realized there were many long-term and happy clients who had benefited from being able to delegate simple tasks and I therefore had years of anecdotal evidence to support what was fast becoming a pretty sound theory. There is value in delegation that can be measured in monetary terms.

In addition, I knew from experience and observation that there were natural barriers to delegation, human nature provides them to a certain degree (trust, control, know-how, guilt) but the art is also restricted by perceived cost and this is particularly relevant in current economic climes and against the backdrop of the assumption that there is value resulting from successful delegation. It would follow that delegation can also be measured as a return on investment, and it follows from that that there is a value in the market that is the *recipient* of delegation.

Th£r£ is valu£ in d£l£gation.

Research

Delegation is a key topic in team development and leadership and is written about expertly and thoroughly by business thinkers and acknowledged gurus in the context of human needs and team motivation.

Its value – which as we have established is inherently measurable – has never been discussed.

Research therefore was begun in the form of an online survey in January 2013 and has remained open ever since. It is open to anyone to complete and promoted online and through the small business community by word of mouth. The variations in delegation value and the proportions of growth expected have come to form a breathing reflection of business confidence in the UK.

In addition, the survey originally intended to identify, now endeavours to affirm attitudes to barriers to delegation as a skill and as a business process.[1]

Findings

Far from the original hope that maybe, just maybe, an amount of delegation would free up sufficient time to enable a 19% growth in the SME market, the result has consistently fluctuated above

---

[1] www.surveymonkey.com/s/theartofdelegation, accessed 10th October 2014.

this level – exceeding my wildest hopes. This fact has driven everything, with impulsion, that results.

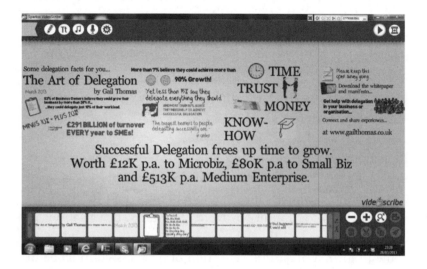

I had believed that the level of growth would be lower and the benefit derived from the difference between cost of delegation and value of growth achieved but that the percentages might be similar and therefore far less impressive than they actually are.

In considering the barriers to delegation, it was expected that cost would be the key issue by far, and in retrospect the survey encouraged this to be the outcome by allowing a question specifically focused on the expense of outsourcing.

This was not the case. In fact, it comes third consistently, after *time*, which is the major issue, and *trust* (and within this control). Barriers therefore prove consistently relatively evenly split.

It was expected that a proportion of respondents would appreciate *assistance* in acquiring the art of delegation in order to delegate successfully. That this would to date not drop below two-thirds of respondents was thoroughly unex pected and further supported the need to develop a range of training products that would help both educationally and vocationally.

It was also proposed, quite early on in the research findings, that the optimism associated with levels of growth presumed to be achievable once workload was delegated fluctuated as a reflection of overall business confidence in this market. For example, in January, a time associated with new year and new hope, expectations were considerably higher than in March, notoriously one of the months associated with business failures as a result of cash-flow problems.

Growth expectations fluctuate with business confidence.

Statistics

The most important statistic to come out of the research is the level of business growth respondents feel is likely if delegation of 10% of their workload could be achieved, and it is very easily calculated once the growth factor is identified.

The key statistics currently measured are listed below (with the figures at time of writing in italics). Commentary on these additional findings and statistics will be published and can be found via http://giftoftime.yourgoalstoday.com/ or www. theartofdelegation.co.uk.

The current value of delegation in the SME market:[2]

*   *£291 billion* per annum.

Number who believe that they could grow their business by more than 20%:

*   *53%* of business owners.

Number who delegate everything they should and could:

*   Less than *15%*.

Number who agree they need help to achieve successful delegation:

*   More than *80%*.

Further activity

Following the identification of clear differences in attitudes to delegation and barriers to it as well as levels of current and prior success, it was clear that to be able to educate people, employees, business owners, civil servants, directors and everyone at large

---

[2] Statistics based on business growth felt achievable by respondents if 10% of workload could be delegated.

on the art of delegation and the benefits it brings, they would need to be spoken to in terms they related to and resonated with.

To this end, 'delegation types' based on barriers and attitudes to delegation were postured, tested and mapped onto Myers–Briggs Personality types to produce 'delegation type indicator profiles', which could then be used to assist with overcoming issues and developing the skill of successful delegation.[3]

The identification of such profiles led to the development of a 'delegation programme' that worked directly with executives and business owners to identify areas of workload which could be delegated (either to process, technology, staff member or out-sourced from the organization entirely).

This work produced case studies with tangible financial measures of saving or additional revenue that could be attributed to the art of delegation and so support the survey results and the fact that successful delegation frees up time which creates higher turnover or profitability through growth or efficiencies.

Case study 1: Gail Thomas and virtual PA company

As the author of the survey, DTI profiles, delegation pro-gramme, White Paper and manifesto and self-appointed

---

[3] Myers–Briggs is a method of personality assessment which is used extensively in team formation to understand how an individual interacts with others and their place in the mix of a team, career or profession. You can find out more here: www.myersbriggs.org.

delegation specialist, it seemed only right that I should prove my own theory and so proceeded to identify and delegate aspects of my own workload so that I would be freed up to grow the business. In doing this, I needed to develop and delegate a sales process to the team in the office. To enable them to receive the sales process for their own business they too needed to free up time and increase efficiency in their operation. Tweaks to their daily regime to achieve this have so far saved some £8k per annum. April 2013 was the month that the new regimen began in earnest and the target was to achieve a 20% uplift in turnover by the end of the year. By July 2013, the business was already 10% up like for like, year on year.

Case study 2: Online gift delivery service start-up

Working with this start-up and looking at its business plan, allowed me to identify that the start-up capital was at risk by virtue of the intention to lease storage capability and purchase stock as part of the proposition that didn't form the USP of the operation (kept unidentified in order to protect the idea at this stage). By outsourcing or delegating the range and fulfil-ment function on a drop ship arrangement, the founders saved some £30k in expenditure, reserving it instead for marketing and working capital.

Other case studies are in progress too and can be found at http://thegiftoftime.yourgoalstoday.com/ and associated blog posts and will continue to be published as they accumulate results to support the financial value in and benefits resulting from delegation.

Conclusion

What the survey, study and case study businesses and business owners and general reaction support is that delegation is an art form or skill that is a key part to success in life, business and career.

A clear indication that respondents saw not only a value in reducing their workload, and a confidence in achieving business growth with the time released, but also a willingness and a need to be guided in their endeavours to achieve it.

Business growth is known to support GDP, employment, job creation, economic prosperity, national confidence, consumer confidence, business start-ups and the development of new products and services. There can be no doubt that it needs to be encouraged.

By accepting the need for education in the art of delegation by respondents, we inadvertently create a market for delegation. Given that the survey and subsequent valuation are based on only 10% of workload being delegated successfully, this valuation – although substantial – is also minimal. In addition, that the base 10% of anyone's workload can be assumed to be largely administrative, it can be assumed that such work can be almost wholly outsourced where resources are not available in-house.

Acceptance of this assumption enables us to presume a conservative value for the outsourced market which most aptly fits the work likely to be delegated: the virtual assistant market. If a 200% return on investment is regarded as acceptable in this calculation, then the VA market can comfortably be valued at well over £1 billion.[4]

---

[4]Based on average client spend with virtual PA company per annum versus turnover difference (i.e. uplift) expected by survey respondents as a result of delegating 10% of workload.

APPENDIX 2: THE ART OF DELEGATION MANIFESTO

The value in delegation calls for action on a number of fronts and actions resulting are summarized in the following strategic outline. It is one which in its overarching capacity supports business growth per se and thus economic recovery and ultimately prosperity.

Education

- schools, colleges of further education, private business schools, vocational training

- licence of VA training to support business start-up syllabus

- licence of delegation training to support business growth and well-being in the workplace agenda.

Valuation and unity of the virtual market

- to raise awareness of outsourcing and ensure minimum 'industry standards' exist.

Industry-standard VA training and accreditation

- to give corporate, government and non-government organizations confidence to support the virtual market rather than ask or expect executives to do work for which they are overqualified.

Training and consultancy in business

- following awareness from a keynote delivery and introduction, a process of workshop training, resources audit and one-to-one coaching and consultancy will be made available to businesses of all sizes.

Virtual PA co franchise to support

- business start-ups

- business growth – through delegation and subcontracting

- (un)employment

- youth (un)employment through apprenticeships and charitable donations of support in kind to selected start-ups

- flexible and part-time working.

Perpetual VA

- to enable self-employed virtual assistants to add to their services available for outsourcing through the provision of wholesale call answering and associate services and resources.

Campaigns

- funding for start-ups

- no VAT for VAs

- reduction of employer's tax liability to encourage employment

- government returns to the taxpayer through effective delegation, communication and structure

- charities and corporations educated to adopt flexible working where possible and benefit from skilled employees currently excluded from the workplace.

ABOUT THE AUTHOR

Having fallen into business studies as a lost soul without the right grades for uni after a mediocre set of A levels results, Gail was bitten by the business bug but afraid to make the leap and start up on her own, so she went and got a job instead. Following an MBA and a FTSE board position, she gave up a successful corporate career at the age of 30, having decided it was time to become a businessperson. The dream was to own or co-own a number (or portfolio) of small businesses, all to be run by an appropriate manager while Gail enjoyed much free time and long holidays. It took fifteen years to achieve the former; she's still working on the latter.

Gail is a happily married, proud mother of two boys and already thinking about the second (and third) book, and maybe a PhD.

And probably another business.

ACKNOWLEDGEMENTS

In business, connections really are important and there a number of links in the connection chain that led me to Sahar Hashemi, who had faith enough in my delegation theory to introduce me to her publisher. I thank all involved in that chain and especially, of course, Sahar.

The team at Wiley are amazing. They make everything easy: Holly Bennion and Vicky Kinsmen kept me encouraged and keen as I worked through the manuscript. Jenny Ng and the ever-patient Tim Bettsworth made the copy-editing journey as smooth as could possibly be.

Naturally, I owe Vince Cable – or his speech-writer – a debt of thanks, as well as all the people who filled out my surveys and tolerated my questioning. I especially thank my clients: I have learnt and continue to learn so much from you all. My business partners and team are the best – I'm so lucky to have you.

A huge motivation 'to only do what only I can do' was my family. I want to be there for my husband and children and in the main I am fortunate to have that privilege. At times, though, my enthusiasm for business gets in the way and they have to do without me. Their love and support are priceless and irreplaceable.

This book is dedicated to the memory of my father – Arthur, a welder of some note in northern parts, who told me, 'Education is a fine thing, use it to find a job you love, because it's a long miserable life if you don't.' I did it, Dad! Also to Charlotte, my first niece, who only got to 12 years old, but who forever helps to fuel my rebellious side and reinforce my resolve to never stop asking questions.

INDEX

INDEX